The Gentle Art of Making Love

Michio Kushi
with
Edward and Wendy Esko

AVERY PUBLISHING GROUP INC.
Garden City Park, New York

The health procedures in this book are based on the training, personal experiences, and research of the author. Because each person and situation is unique, the editor and publisher urge the reader to check with a qualified health professional before using any procedure where there is any question as to its appropriateness.

The publisher does not advocate the use of any particular diet and exercise program, but believes the informaton presented in this book should be available to the public. If you have a history of back troubles, or other physical restrictions, we recommend that you consult with your health care provider before beginning any exercise program.

Because there is always some risk involved, the author and publisher are not responsible for any adverse effects or consequences resulting from the use of any of the suggestions, preparations, or procedures in this book. Please do not use the book if you are unwilling to assume the risk. Feel free to consult a physician or other qualified health professional. It is a sign of wisdom, not cowardice, to seek a second or third opinion.

Text illustrations by Michael Apice
In-house editor: Karen Price
Typesetting by Multifacit Graphics, Inc.

Library of Congress Cataloging-in-Publication Data

Kushi, Michio.
    The gentle art of making love: macrobiotics in love and sexuality
    /Michio Kushi with Edward and Wendy Esko.
       p.   cm.
    Includes bibliographical references.
    ISBN 0-89529-435-4
    1. Sex (Biology)—Nutritional aspects. 2. Macrobiotic diet.
    3. Massage. I. Esko, Edward. II. Esko, Wendy. III. Title.
    RA788.K87 1990
    613.9'6—dc20   90-30829
                                                    CIP

Printed in the United States of America

10 9 8 7 6 5 4 3 2 1

Contents

Preface,   v

1. Making Love: Why Opposites Attract,   1
2. Food and Sex: A Logical Connection,   21
3. Massage for Couples,   51
4. Solving Sexual Problems,   75
5. Recipes for Healthy Sexuality,   125

Afterword,   189
For Further Study,   193
Index,   195

Preface

After nearly forty years of married life, there are still many things about the relationship between men and women that are a mystery to me. Often, when my wife, Aveline, and I return home from a lecture, she will say, "Michio, what you said tonight was wrong. Why did you say such a foolish thing?" I have discovered that because of their complexity, the best thing to do is to accept these mysteries and cope with them joyfully in our daily lives.

What is the purpose of relationships between men and women? Is it only to have children, to enjoy sex, or to share life's experiences? Each of us has come to this life from the infinite universe, taking millions of years and changing ourselves from one level of existence to the next, and finally appearing as a human being on the earth. Our heritage is the memory that we were once infinite, universal existence, and so naturally each of us, without exception, seeks unconditional love, happiness, and peace. As human beings, we begin the return journey to infinity, led by the memory of our universal origin.

All things have yin and yang, or male and female, as their basis of existence. And what do yin and yang strive to achieve? These opposites are continuously seeking oneness, beyond male and female, plus and minus, or yin and yang. So once people reach physical maturity, they seek the opposite sex to achieve harmony with the ever-changing, relative world.

Relationships between men and women often begin at the

physical level, but this is only a small, though basic, part of achieving oneness. The real purpose of relationships is to refine and harmonize our consciousness, to achieve a state beyond male or female, by uniting with our opposite. The ultimate goal is spiritual harmony, and to achieve this takes a whole lifetime.

In this book, we discuss relationships on their most basic level. We explain love and sexuality in terms of universal attraction and energy, and describe the physical and energetic reactions that occur when two people make love. We also discuss the logical connection between food and sex, and explain how what takes place in the bedroom is often the outcome of what we do in the kitchen.

We also present a basic massage routine, designed to strengthen physical and sexual vitality and enhance sensitivity and communication between couples. Also included is the macrobiotic dietary and way-of-life approach to common sexual problems, including impotence, premature ejaculation, and difficulty with orgasm.

It is my hope that *The Gentle Art of Making Love* will guide couples toward physical, mental, and spiritual health and harmony, both now and in the future.

I would like to thank Edward Esko for compiling and editing the material for this book from my Kushi Institute lectures on Love, Sex, and Macrobiotics, and for preparing the final draft. I also thank Wendy Esko for compiling the recipes from the cooking classes and seminars presented by my wife, Aveline. I would also like to thank Rudy Shur and the staff of Avery Publishing Group for their guidance in preparing this book.

Michio Kushi
Brookline, Massachusetts

1.

Making Love: Why Opposites Attract

The mysteries of love can be explained in very simple terms. Everything in the universe has its opposite: day exists with night, inside with outside, and man with woman. Throughout history, people in different parts of the world have recognized this, and have classified all things into two complementary categories which we call **yin** and **yang**. Although these terms were first used thousands of years ago in China, the understanding they represent is not particularly Oriental. A similar understanding can be found in all of the world's great cultures.

YIN AND YANG

Life moves rhythmically, and yin and yang describe this rhythmic movement. Yin represents the centrifugal, expanding, or upward energy or movement; and yang, the centripetal, contracting, and downward energy or movement. Since all things are continually in motion, yin and yang are present in everything; however, some things have a more yin or expansive tendency, and others a more yang or contracting tendency. All things come and go, appear and disappear, and move and change because of the interaction of these primary forces.

Love and sex are examples of yin and yang, as are other daily rhythms such as waking and sleeping, appetite and fullness, and movement and rest. These activities occur in the form of waves—for example, sexual tension builds up and is then released, and then builds up again. At certain times we feel romantically inclined, and at others, less so. This pattern is similar to the coming and going of the tides, the waxing and waning of the moon, and the changing of the seasons.

Like the opposite poles of a magnet, the opposite energies of yin and yang attract one another. Similarly, two yin energies have a tendency to repel, as do two yang energies. At its most basic level, human sexuality is a form of interplay between these universal forces.

Yin and Yang appear on our planet as the forces of heaven and earth. **Earth's force** spirals out from the spinning globe back to the universe. Earth's energy is more yin—upward and expansive. Spiraling in from infinite space, **heaven's force** is the opposite. It includes cosmic rays, radiation, solar energy, air pressure, and so on. Its elements converge toward the planet. Its direction is downward, inward, and contracting, and we classify it as more yang.

If you hang a nail clipper on a thread and hold it over a man's head, it will move in a counterclockwise circle. Do the same over a woman's head and the clipper will move clockwise. What this means is that men and women have opposite energies. Men receive more of heaven's downward energy (which spirals counterclockwise in the northern hemisphere), and women, more of the earth's rising power (which spirals clockwise). (See Figure 1.1.) If the man and woman touch, the clipper stops moving. This is because their opposite energies cancel each other out, creating a balanced condition. This balanced condition is what we seek when we make love.

Nothing can exist by one force alone. For instance, if something were created only by heaven's force, it would contract to an infinitely small point and disappear. If something were created by earth's force only, it would expand to an infinitely large size and would also cease to exist. Everything contains both yin and yang combined. However, some things have a greater degree of heaven's force, and others, a larger proportion of earth's force. Men and women are perfect examples.

When one human being is constituted more by heaven's force and another by earth's, they are attracted to each other.

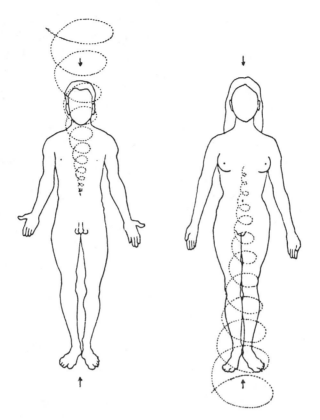

Figure 1.1   Heaven's Force in Man and Earth's Force in Woman.

These opposites fall in love and want to be together. When we say, "I love you" and can't stop thinking about our partner, the "I" that is saying this is a reflection of the attraction between heaven and earth. For men, it represents heaven's force loving or being attracted to a woman's earth's force. For women, it represents earth's force seeking to become one with the opposite force of heaven.

Actually, when we talk about love it is not just men and women that we are talking about, but the forces of heaven and earth that are powerfully charging them. A man's character and a woman's charm and their sexuality and consciousness are generated by heaven and earth. So the degree and quality of heaven's force that the man manifests, and of the earth's force that the woman personifies, determine the degree of attraction, called love, or repulsion, called dislike, that arises between a couple.

Human sexuality can be better understood with an example from nature. From the earth a tree branches upward, under the influence of the earth's more expansive energy. Clouds passing overhead during a thunderstorm carry an opposite charge, having condensed under the influence of heaven's contracting energy. As the clouds gather, humidity becomes thick, causing the atmosphere to become electrically conductive. Tension increases and soon a powerful charge passes between clouds and tree, followed by the loud clap of thunder. A tremendous amount of energy has been released. Once the storm passes, the atmosphere becomes peaceful and quiet, with a calmness like that of contented lovers.

The flash of lightning is similar to the release of energy that occurs during sex. The female body conducts more of the earth's force, like the tree, and the male body, more of heaven's force. And between the two a spark arises. Men seek women and women seek men just as other pairs of opposites attract. Yin can't exist by itself, and neither can yang. Through love and sex, human beings unite with their opposite energies. Each person becomes more whole or complete.

During intercourse, men and women connect at the genital region. The genital regions are oppositely charged energy poles, and when connected these energies become one. This connection is something that is done intuitively. Intuition means our native understanding that opposites attract and likes repel. With our intuition we seek warmth on a cold day or want to drink fluids after eating something salty. Similarly, we don't light a fire in the fireplace on a steamy July day, nor do we continue eating after we are full.

Couples instinctively know that in order to neutralize their built-up energies they must increase the intensity of that energy. This can be accomplished in a variety of ways, most often by rhythmic motion. As the intensity becomes greater, energy comes in stronger and stronger waves. This gradually creates a very high level of tension. Finally, at its peak, a spark like thunder and lightning passes through their bodies. Then the forces of heaven and earth cancel each other out and the pair becomes balanced. This is sex.

With their excessive male and female qualities neutralized, the couple no longer needs to connect their energy poles. Then, maybe several days later, or in some cases several hours later, an excessive charge again begins to accumulate and again they connect their magnetic poles.

Actually, love is not complicated at all. It is simply a reflection of universal energy. Although Romeo and Juliet thought they were special, their passion was merely a reflection of the cosmic dance between heaven and earth.

THE CHAKRA RESPONSE

Thousands of years ago, people understood that human beings were made up of more than just skin, bones, cells, and bodily fluids. They understood that there was a life force that could not be seen. We can think of this undefinable quality as the energy of life itself. This invisible force was given names such as *Ki* in Japan, *Ch'i* in China, and *prana* in India. These terms are still in use today, as are arts based on the use of this energy. Acupuncture, for example, is based on adjusting the body's energy in order to establish balance or health. The traditional practices of chanting and meditation are also built on this principle. Making love is simply a natural way to bring human energy into harmony with the universe.

Energy flows through the body in the same way that water flows from a mighty river into many small branches or streams. The central energy stream runs deep inside the body from the top of the head to the sexual organ. It is the primary channel for the flow of heaven and earth's forces through the body and supplies energy to the **meridians**, which are invisible currents of energy that run just below the skin. The central energy stream also supplies energy to the organs, tissues, and cells. Each cell is actually a highly charged energy center.

There are also seven focal points of energy located along the primary channel. In ancient India, these energy centers were referred to as the seven **chakras** or "wheels" of energy. The

cells, tissues, organs, and meridians feed into and are nourished by the chakras and primary channel, and, ultimately, by
the forces of heaven and earth. Refer to Figure 1.2 for the
locations of the chakras.

When people make love, the charge of energy along the
primary channel intensifies, activating and vitalizing each of
the chakras and the functions they nourish. The spark that
occurs during orgasm flows through the primary channel,
charging each chakra with an energy that radiates throughout
the body. Because sex involves activation of the body's energy
system, with the chakras as the primary focus, we may refer to
it as the **chakra response**.

The primary channel is the main pathway for the forces of
heaven and earth. Heaven's force spirals in from the universe
and enters the top of the head in the region of the hair spiral,
or cowlick. This highly charged place is known as the **crown** or
seventh chakra. It supplies energy to the cerebral cortex, activating the images, consciousness, and sensations that arise
there.

After entering the head, heaven's force intensively charges
the innermost region of the brain—the area of the midbrain.
From this region, known as the **sixth chakra**, energy is distributed to other parts of the brain, sending electromagnetic influences to the millions of cells in the brain. Brain cells operate as
highly communicative instruments, processing vibrations in a
manner similar to a television set, receiving energy from the
primary channel and producing images, sensations, and
consciousness.

The most natural position for a couple to make love in is for
the man to be above and the woman below. This is because the
male body is charged more with heaven's force, which comes
down upon the earth, and the female body conducts more of
earth's force, which moves up from the planet toward space.
Because heaven's force enters at the head spiral, man's upper
chakras are strongly charged and active during sex. It is
through activation of the midbrain chakra that partners, and
especially the male, are able to control the speed and intensity
of their lovemaking.

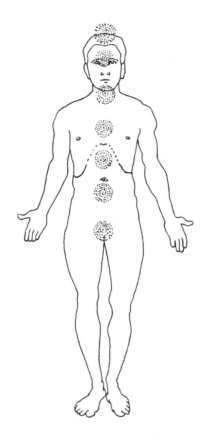

Figure 1.2   The Location of the Seven Chakras.

In women, the pole that is opposite to the man's highly activated upper chakras is called the **hara chakra**. This is located deep within the uterus and is strongly charged and active. Of course, both sexes have each of these areas charged, but of the two regions, one is more strongly activated by earth and the other more by heaven. For this reason, man's sexual activity is strongly influenced by his imagination, so he is able to engage in sex with a woman without feeling love for her. A woman usually needs more total, physical, and tangible love. Unless she feels loved, it is difficult for her to enter into a sexual relationship.

The chakra response normally begins in the upper body and gradually proceeds to the lower energy centers. Sensory arousal follows a similar pattern, beginning with the purely vibrational senses of sight and hearing, which have their focus in the head, and progressing to the more physical sense of touch, which involves the body. When partners find each other attractive, these messages are relayed to the midbrain, where they create impulses that activate the meridians, organs, and endocrine glands, especially the pituitary. Activation of the pituitary gland stimulates secretion of gonadotropic hormones which in turn cause the reproductive organs to secrete sex hormones.

Visual attraction alternates between seeing a person's totality—including their actions and behavior—and concentrating on specific aspects of their character and appearance. It normally combines with another more subtle form of chakra exchange in which a man and a woman "sense" each other's energy. The quality of each person's energy determines whether or not they are attracted to one another. Compatibility occurs when one person's energy is especially complementary to another's.

The vibrations of speech originate in the **fifth** or **throat chakra**. The quality of these vibrations helps determine the other person's response. Soft, romantic expressions relax and open the chakras, causing them to become active. Gentle words of love whispered between partners help activate the chakra response. Loud noises or harsh expressions make the chakras constrict and tighten, diminishing the flow of energy through them and causing their responsiveness to fade.

When partners touch, they exchange energy directly from body to body. Touching sends sensory impulses through the nerve endings to the midbrain and transmits energy directly through the meridians just below the skin. As a result, any part of the body can become an erogenous zone if the proper stimulation is provided. Touching may also activate the **secondary chakras**, energy centers located in the center of both palms. These chakras send energy to, and receive it from, the primary channel, especially the heart chakra in the center of the chest. When couples hold hands or press their palms together, these secondary chakras channel energy from heart to heart, stimulating feelings of warmth and closeness.

Kissing is an intimate form of touch. The lips, tongue, and other parts of the mouth are highly sensitive to touch and convey impulses directly to the midbrain. Saliva carries a strong electromagnetic charge, as do the fluids secreted by the sexual organs during arousal. Erotic kissing sends impulses through the primary channel directly to the sexual organs. As with the hands and fingers, the lips and tongue can be used to stimulate the flow of energy and generate sensory awareness in any part of the body.

The **fourth** or **heart chakra** is located in the center of the chest. Here, the active rhythm of heaven and earth's forces produces the heartbeat. Contracting of the heart is produced by heaven's force, and expansion by earth's force. The rhythmic movement of the lungs is also regulated by the energy in this chakra. Feelings and emotions, especially those of love, compassion, and tenderness, are also generated here.

The physical desire to merge with your partner is centered in the lower body, especially in the hara chakra. The desire to merge mentally and spiritually is centered in the midbrain. Earth's force causes the energy (and feelings) generated in the hara to move upward along the primary channel, while heaven's force causes the vibrations produced by images in the brain to move downward. These forces merge in the heart chakra, producing full active energy that stimulates the heart and nerve endings that connect with it, causing actual physical sensations.

Since ancient times, the heart has been associated with love. The songs, poems, and sayings of every culture refer to it as the center of love and tenderness. These associations are based on actual feelings. Falling in love is often felt as a sensation of lightness, expansion, or fullness centered around the heart. Separation from a loved one can produce a sensation of longing or aching in the heart region, symbolized in modern expressions such as "heartache" or "heartbreak." This chakra creates the aspiration to love or become one with another person, as well as anticipation and excitement at the possibility of achieving this desire.

These feelings intensify during the embrace. In this act, men and women open their arms and extend their hearts toward one another. Their breathing tends to focus in the chest. This position opens the heart chakra and generates strong feelings of love. When lovers embrace, they bring their heart chakras into direct contact, giving or "surrendering" these vibrations to the other person while "opening" the chakra in order to receive them. They can also feel the other person's heartbeat. Expressions such as "giving" or "opening" one's heart symbolize this loving exchange. The emotional bonding that occurs is heightened when the partners look softly into each other's eyes, kiss, and gently caress one another.

As the chakra response intensifies, heartbeat and breathing accelerate. In both sexes, the heart rate can accelerate to over twice the normal rate as orgasm approaches, and blood pressure can rise by as much as a third. The rate of breathing can also become several times faster than normal.

Activation of the heart and other chakras produces a reaction in a woman's breasts. The nipples may become erect and the breasts may increase in size. This reaction is stimulated by gentle touching, caressing, or kissing, accelerating the flow of energy and creating higher levels of arousal. This is often felt as a light, tingling sensation that spreads throughout the body.

The **third** or **stomach chakra** is located in the center of the solar plexus. It activates the movement of the stomach and digestive organs and supplies the liver, spleen, and kidneys with energy. This chakra also translates the images and feelings generated in the upper chakras into the movements of the lower body. As sex progresses, the stomach chakra stimulates the liver to release glycogen, which is converted to glucose in the bloodstream. This provides the extra energy needed by the cells during active sex. Moreover, the stomach chakra stimulates the spleen to contract, making more blood available to the circulatory system, increasing the capacity to absorb oxygen.

The differences between men and women are most apparent in the lower body. The sexual organs develop during the embryonic period when the influences of heaven and earth first become apparent. The uvula is created by heaven's downward

Love Meditation

Meditation can be used to enhance the love between partners. In this simple exercise, we generate the flow of energy in the chest region, producing active feelings of love and harmony that radiate outward from the heart chakra. To practice love meditation, do the following.

1. *Sit on a chair or on the floor facing each other. You may sit in the cross-legged position or with the legs and feet tucked under the buttocks as in Figure 1.3. Keep your spine naturally straight and let your hands rest comfortably in your lap. Close your eyes and breathe naturally and quietly for about a minute.*

**Figure 1.3　Partners Seated in Preparation for Love
Meditation.**

2. *Then, open your eyes halfway and begin looking gently into each other's eyes.*

3. *Slowly open both arms wide as if ready to accept and embrace your partner, as in Figure 1.4. Keep both hands naturally opened toward the front, as illustrated, with no tension.*

4. *Start to breathe with your chest, especially at the area of the heart, with a long, gentle inhalation that is slightly longer than the exhalation. Keep your mouth slightly open as you breathe this way. Also, as you breathe in, move your chest slightly forward as if your body is starting to glide toward your partner. As you gently breathe out, let your body naturally return to the normal position.*

Figure 1.4   Accepting Your Partner with Open Arms.

5. *Continue in this rhythm for about five minutes, during which you may silently repeat the words "love" and "harmony" in your mind.*
6. *To finish love meditation, return your hands to the original position in your lap, close your eyes, and return your breathing to normal. Sit quietly for about a minute before concluding.*

force. Men and women both develop one, but in the male embryo, the stronger charge of heaven's force causes a similar organ to appear in a larger form in the lower body. We refer to this organ as the penis.

The female embryo receives more of earth's upward energy and does not develop such an extended organ in the lower body. Instead, a smaller organ, the clitoris, appears. Earth's rising energy causes the female sexual organs to develop in a more upward direction inside the body, while in the male, heaven's force causes them to appear outside the body in a more downward position. The vagina, uterus, and ovaries are positioned opposite to the penis, scrotum, and testes.

Earth's force continues up through the body, and in the chest branches into a pair of spirals that develop into nipples. Baby girls and boys both have them, and it is not until puberty that estrogen and other female hormones cause the female breasts to enlarge. These hormones are more yin and are charged primarily by the expanding energy of the earth. The male hormone testosterone has an opposite quality. Boys don't develop expanded breasts, but instead develop more yang, masculine characteristics such as facial hair.

Male and female sexual organs are opposite to each other in structure, position, and the type of energy they conduct. These differences provide the basis for sexual attraction and lovemaking.

During sex, the **second** or **hara chakra** becomes very highly charged, as does the **first** or **sexual chakra** in the pubic region.

The hara chakra is located in the lower part of the small intestine and is the central focus of energy in the lower abdomen. It is also referred to as *Ki-Kai*, or "ocean of electromagnetic energy," and *Tan-Den*, or the "central field" of energy. From here energy is distributed in waves, causing rhythmic expansion and contraction of the small and large intestines. Intestinal digestion, decomposition and absorption of food molecules, and movement of the intestines become possible due to the energy flowing from this chakra.

In women, the hara chakra is located in the upper part of the uterus. Should fertilization occur, it is here that implantation of the fertilized ovum takes place. The intense charge of life energy in this region stimulates development of the placenta and embryo, and after nine months activates the contractions that occur during labor. Labor begins when the charge of heaven and earth's forces intensifies in the hara region, causing the uterus to begin rhythmic contractions. These movements normally begin in the hara chakra and spread downward in the form of a wave. During intercourse, similar, although milder, uterine contractions may occur when energy peaks at the moment of orgasm.

The gathering of heaven's force in a man's lower body and chakras accelerates the flow of blood to the penis, causing it to enlarge and become erect. Heaven's force also energizes the testes, causing them to enlarge, and during intercourse stimulates the man to begin rhythmically moving his lower body back and forth. The prostate gland also receives energy, but reacts in a way that is opposite to the penis. As it becomes more highly charged it contracts, while the buildup of energy in the penis causes that organ to expand.

In women, sexual arousal follows intensification of earth's force along the primary channel and in the chakras. As earth's force gathers in the pelvic region, the lips of the vagina expand and open and the vaginal walls secrete a highly charged fluid. The vagina also enlarges, but in a way that is opposite to the penis. The inner portions of the vagina expand inward toward the cervix. The clitoris also becomes highly charged and sensitized, and functions in a way that is complementary to the vagina. As earth's force gathers in the sexual chakra, the clitoris eventually contracts, while earth's force causes the vagina to open and expand.

During foreplay, the continual buildup of heaven's and earth's forces in both partners causes the desire for physical union. Sexual union creates a complete circuit of these primary energies. With the woman on her back and the man on top, heaven's force enters his crown chakra, flows through the length of the primary channel, and exits through the penis. It enters the woman's body through the vagina, flows up through her primary channel, and exits through her crown chakra. Earth's force simultaneously enters her body at the crown chakra, especially when she presses the back of her head downward, passes through her body to the vagina, and enters the man's penis. It flows up along his primary channel and exits through his crown chakra.

As the movements of intercourse intensify, energy from the cells, organs, and meridians gathers toward the chakras and primary channel, causing the muscles to contract. When energy flows inward from the hands and fingers, it may cause the hands and fingers to curl slightly. When it flows up from the feet toward the hara chakra it may cause the toes to slightly curl. As energy gathers toward the center of the body, the muscles of the face, neck, and buttocks may also contract. Both partners also start to move in concert with one another: as the man moves his pelvis downward, the woman responds by moving her's upward to meet him.

The concentration of heaven's force in the penis is accelerated by contact with the energized vagina. In a similar way, the concentration of earth's force in a woman's lower body is heightened by the presence of the highly charged penis. Both partners experience this as an intense sensation of pleasure that gathers toward the sexual organs. This pleasure is heightened by gentle movement.

As orgasm approaches, additional blood and energy gather in the penis causing the tip, or glans, to enlarge further. Counterbalancing this, energy gathers in the vagina, causing it to envelop the penis more tightly. The intensification of energy in the hara and sexual chakras can also cause the uterus and testicles to move upward.

Finally, as the concentration of energy reaches its peak, the man is no longer able to consciously control the downward rush of heaven's force along the primary channel. Orgasm is now inevitable as each chakra begins releasing uncontrollable waves of energy. As energy pours from the chakras, the testes, prostate, and seminal vesicles begin automatically contracting, collecting sperm and seminal fluid and discharging them into the urethra. Then, the contracting wave spreads outward along the length of the penis, carrying the sperm and seminal fluid with it. These contractions last for several seconds and then diminish.

In the female body, earth's force continously builds up in each of the chakras and gathers in the uterus, vagina, labia, and clitoris. When this buildup reaches a peak, energy pours from each chakra in waves, producing uncontrollable contractions in the outer portion of the vagina. A wave of contractions may also start at the top of the uterus in the location of the hara chakra and spread downward along the length of the organ. These contracting movements last for a moment and then subside.

ORGASM AND BEYOND

Understanding the nature of heaven and earth's forces helps explain why men and women experience orgasm differently, and how their experiences complement each other.

Heaven's force produces a concentration of energy that rapidly builds and dissipates. These characteristics are reflected in the male drive to achieve orgasm, and as intercourse progresses, in the concentration of male sensory focus in the penis.

Earth's force produces opposite characteristics. In general, the motion generated by the earth is slower and longer lasting than that produced by heaven. Earth's force also creates diffusion, in contrast to the concentration of energy produced by heaven's force. As a result, a woman's sensory focus is often more diffused during sex. It may encompass the vagina, clitoris, labia, and pelvis as a whole. Because it takes longer for this wider area to become fully charged, a woman usually needs more time for the chakra response to build. However, once energy builds to the level of orgasm, a woman can sustain the experience longer than a man and is often able to enjoy multiple orgasms.

Men normally have the tendency to progress rapidly toward orgasm, while women move more gradually toward higher and higher levels of sensory experience. A man often experiences the greatest release of energy in his first orgasm—especially if it follows a period of sexual inactivity— while a woman often finds her second or third orgasm more intense and satisfying than the first.

A feeling that orgasm is inevitable is experienced as the chakras release energy a moment before physical contractions begin. Both partners may experience their bodies tensing up as they prepare for the sudden release of chakra energy and the physical contractions that follow.

The eruption of chakra energy in the man causes the prostate to begin contracting, as seminal fluid gathers toward the urethra. This is followed by a wave of contractions that carry the sperm outward along the penis. Men often experience this together with deep and rapid vibrations felt at the core of their being. These vibrations produce sensations along the length of the primary channel as the chakras are united in one flowing pulse of energy. A man may momentarily lose awareness of his physical body and feel as if he is merging with his partner and with the pulsating energy of heaven and earth.

Women experience waves of contractions that begin in the outer part of the vagina and sometimes in the uterus. Their sensory focus, initially concentrated in the clitoris, vagina, and labia, begins to radiate upward through the pelvis and then along the primary channel. She may experience this as a deep vibration or "throbbing" that spreads upward and merges with the heartbeat. As this rising pulse of energy reaches the heart chakra, it generates intense feelings of warmth, love, and acceptance that radiate outward from the core of her being toward her partner and to the universe beyond. Ideally, as these feelings reach a peak, her partner will ejaculate a stream of highly charged sperm deep within the vagina.

At this moment of peak intensity, both partners merge into one pulsating, harmonious rhythm that vibrates together with heaven and earth. They experience a harmony and completeness like that of the infinite universe itself, as if the two halves of infinity have found each other and have finally reunited. From the depth of their souls, an overwhelming sense of gratitude may spring forth for the profound mystery of creation that brought them to each other.

Sometimes this fusion is powerful enough to create new life. After entering the vagina, sperm are aided in their motion by the invisible, upward current of earth's force that continually streams along the woman's primary channel. During their journey, sperm travel upward through the vagina, the uterus, and into the Fallopian tubes. Only several hundred of the several hundred million sperm ejaculated in the vagina reach the far end of the Fallopian tubes, where, if a mature egg has been released from the ovary, one will penetrate the outer surface of the egg and fertilize it.

The fertilized ovum carries within it an unlimited potential for future development. The egg and sperm that unite both contain a complete record of the evolution of life, together with a vision of, and aspiration toward, an unending future. At the moment of conception, a new human being is created that embodies both of these aspects and that fuses the qualities of both parents into one.

A tremendous amount of energy has been released. As the chakras begin to "cool," the bodily changes created by the chakra response gradually return to normal. Muscle tension and congestion in the blood vessels dissipate, and the sexual organs gradually return to their prearoused state. A man's charge of energy cools off more quickly, especially the charge of energy centered around the midbrain. A woman's center, the hara, is deep within her body and doesn't cool off so quickly. Once again there is a difference, a complementary reaction between the two.

At this time, each partner can express love and care for the other by holding, caressing, looking tenderly into each other's eyes, and together sharing the afterglow of chakra energy. In this way, both experience a sense of joy and completeness, sharing the sublime feeling of harmony with each other and with the whole universe. The flower of human sexuality can then blossom into a love that embraces everything.

2.

Food and Sex: A Logical Connection

The attraction of opposites is everywhere. The invisible force that brings a man and a woman together to share love is the same force that makes the earth rotate, the sun shine, and the flowers blossom. Actually, love is something that we all should know about intuitively, like eating. When we look at nature, we see that birds, flowers, and bees all manage this aspect of life without complicated techniques or elaborate theories. Humans should be able to do this, too.

Sex is the physical exchange that results from this attraction of opposites. It is a form of communication that involves many levels of interaction. The chakra response mentioned in Chapter One activates body, mind, and spirit. Couples who understand each other and are able to communicate are usually sexually happy because they are sensitive and respond to each other's needs. When understanding and communication are present, the differences between men and women become a source of happiness and satisfaction. When these important aspects are missing, conflict and frustration arise.

Without love, the goal of sex is one-sided. It can easily become a mechanical act devoid of emotion or spirituality. If a man does not love the woman he is with, he may not consider her needs. If a woman does not love and trust her partner, she may end up feeling unsatisfied and unfulfilled. Love enables men and women to transcend their immediate desires and achieve more complete harmony, and elevates sexuality to sublime levels of psychic and spiritual interaction. It harmonizes differences and makes antagonisms become complementary. Satisfying sex depends on the health and vitality of both partners. Whether the chakras are able to generate sufficient energy, and the degree to which they charge the entire body, is a function of our physical condition and state of health. Sexuality depends on the smooth flow of heaven and earth's forces through the primary channel and on the capacity of each chakra to generate enough energy to produce the physical responses that lead to orgasm. The ability to communicate with each other also depends on the unblocked flow of energy. If we want to understand the factors that create sexual harmony, therefore, we need to begin with an understanding of what enhances the flow of energy in the body as well as what interferes with it. The most important area to consider is diet.

DIET AND THE CHAKRA RESPONSE

Food is a condensed form of energy. Like everything else, we can understand food in terms of yin and yang, or expansion and contraction, and this can help us see the profound influence it has on sexuality. All foods can be classified according to the type of energy they represent. Some foods have very condensed or contracting energy, others are very expansive, and others are more balanced or centered. The energy that we receive from food has a direct influence on the chakras and the physical responses that occur during sex.

Meat, eggs, chicken, cheese, and other animal foods are very condensed. They are rich in sodium and other contractive minerals and contain hard saturated fat. Nutritionally, their primary components are protein and fat, or in the case of dairy products, calcium and other minerals. These nutrients create the more yang physical structure of the body. The animals from which these foods are taken are ultimately nourished by the plant world. They represent the condensation of a tremendous volume of plant foods. Animal foods are strongly charged with downward or contracting energy and are considered extremely yang. Eating a large volume of meat, eggs, and other animal foods produces constriction and stagnation in the body. The saturated fat and cholesterol contained in animal foods are major causes of the buildup of fatty deposits that clog the arteries and blood vessels and diminish the free flow of blood, producing a condition of sluggishness or stagnation.

Sugar, tropical fruits, spices, coffee, chocolate, tropical vegetables, alcohol, and drugs or medications have more extreme yin or expansive effects. The simple sugars contained in many of these foods are used by the body primarily to generate quick energy. Simple sugars are rapidly absorbed into the bloodstream and are quickly metabolized. Rapid diffusion and decomposition are both yin tendencies. Many of these foods also contain plenty of water. Water dilutes substances, causing them to dissolve and melt. It produces swelling and expansion.

Vegetable foods are, on the whole, more yin or expansive. They are rich in potassium and other expansive elements, and with few exceptions, contain a liquid form of unsaturated fat or oil, in contrast with the more yang saturated fat found in animal foods.

Female sexuality depends upon the smooth flow of upward, yin energy in the body. At the moment of orgasm, sensations originating in the vagina and clitoris radiate up through the pelvis and along the primary channel to the upper chakras. Animal foods are strongly charged with the opposite or downward (yang) energy, and when eaten in excess inhibit the natural unfolding of upward energy in the female body. Animal foods tighten and constrict the chakras and can limit the range of pleasure and depth of emotion that a woman experiences during sex. They can also restrict the focus of sexual pleasure to a more narrow area in the lower body, without the more complete involvement of the upper chakras. Overintake of animal foods can also cause the vagina, which is strongly charged with earth's expanding energy, to become less sensitive to erotic stimulation. This is a leading cause of the inability to achieve orgasm during intercourse.

In men, the overintake of animal foods accelerates the concentration of sexual energy in the lower body, especially in the prostate gland and sexual chakra. This buildup of energy produces the urge for quick, sometimes explosive, release, with less activity in the upper chakras. This is a leading cause of premature ejaculation, or the inability to control the release of chakra energy, and of the tendency to concentrate on orgasm without the more total involvement of the mind and emotions.

Animal foods are not the only extremes that interfere with sexuality. Extreme yin or expansive foods, such as sugar, milk, soft drinks, ice cream, chocolate, and tropical fruits, deplete energy in the primary channel and chakras. This makes it harder to generate and sustain the buildup of sexual energy. Overintake of these foods diminishes physical vitality and sexual appetite. Extreme yin foods tend to affect men more rapidly than they do women, since male sexuality depends more on the strong downward movement of energy in the body. Overconsumption of sugar and other strong yin foods offsets this downward movement, and can produce impotence and premature ejaculation. These foods make it more difficult for a man to concentrate and hold energy in the lower body, especially in the prostate gland. When this happens, it becomes harder to achieve or maintain an erection or control the release of energy during sex. Drugs, including marijuana, cocaine, and others, also weaken sexuality. They are far more extreme than sugar: they can cause sexual potency to disappear and can negatively affect reproductive abilities.

SATURATED FAT AND SEXUALITY

For many people in the modern world, fat is a major part of the diet. It accounts for as much as 42 percent of daily intake, according to some surveys, and a large percentage is eaten in the form of hard, saturated fat. The relationship between a high-fat diet and heart disease and cancer is becoming increasingly well known. However, less well known are the effects of high-fat diets on sexuality. Let us now take a look at how overintake of fat, and saturated fat in particular, influences this aspect of our lives.

Animal foods contain plenty of hard saturated fat and cholesterol. When eaten excessively, these factors accumulate and cause hardening or stagnation. When this happens in the arteries and blood vessels, the result is heart disease. But beyond affecting the blood vessels, saturated fat also produces varying degrees of hardening throughout the body, including the skin, internal organs, chakras, and along the primary channel. When men and women eat plenty of eggs, butter, poultry, and meat, the accumulation of fat and cholesterol throughout the body may cause them to lose conductivity to the forces of heaven and earth. The body as a whole may start to become rigid and inflexible and the skin may become hard, tough, and insensitive, especially to more subtle forms of touch. These conditions interfere with sexuality and with our sensitivity in general.

The reason that the skin becomes rigid and inflexible is that the blood vessels, skin, and other tissues are composed of collagen and elastin, the primary proteins that make up the body's connective tissues. Elastin provides flexibility, softness, and elasticity to the skin, while collagen imparts the toughness that holds it together. When the diet is high in animal foods that contain saturated fat and cholesterol, a variety of things happen to these tissues. When eaten excessively, these foods can cause the ratio of collagen and elastin to gradually shift. A diet high in animal foods causes a gradual depletion of elastin, so that collagen (which is tougher or more yang) becomes more prevalent. As a result, the skin loses its normal flexibility and eventually becomes hard and inelastic.

Overconsumption of fat also accelerates a process known as "cross-linking," in which collagen changes from a soluble to an insoluble form. In children, for example, collagen exists in a flexible form and is made up of short cables that are distinct from each other. The breakdown of fats in the body releases free radicals, which are highly volatile, destructive bits of matter that damage tissues. These stray molecules wedge between the collagen cables, causing them to gradually clump together and become knotted with tough fibers. The result is stiffening, hardening, and loss of elasticity in the skin. As the skin becomes tight and contracted, moisture and natural oils no longer flow smoothly to the surface, producing an overly dry condition.

In both sexes, the skin plays an important role in generating the chakra response and as a focus of sensual pleasure. Energy from the environment constantly enters the body through the skin and travels along the meridians to the chakras, energizing and vitalizing them. At the same time, energy generated internally is discharged along the meridians and out through the skin. Our vitality and sensitivity, and therefore our sexuality, depends on the smooth flow of energy along these pathways. Someone in this condition may also begin to feel cut off from the environment, including other people, and this can lead to a false sense of isolation and an increasingly self-centered approach to relationships.

Overintake of animal fats also affects the activity of the sweat and sebaceous glands in the skin. The gradual cross-linking of collagen accelerated by free radical damage causes these glands to constrict and become less active. Saturated fats also accumulate in the glands and sweat ducts, similar to the way they accumulate in the blood vessels. These conditions block the secretion of moisture and oil that normally keeps the skin smooth and soft. If the skin does not receive enough moisture, it becomes hard, dry, and cracks easily.

The skin is richly supplied with blood vessels. When saturated fat and cholesterol accumulate in these blood vessels, the skin receives less blood, as well as less oxygen and nutrients. Cells depend on oxygen and nutrients for life. If the supply of these vital factors diminishes, cells take longer to renew themselves. The speed at which new skin cells form in the lowest layer of the epidermis and migrate out to the surface of the body decreases. A dull, flaky film develops on the surface of the body as dead, dehydrated cells accumulate rather than being quickly sloughed off and replaced by new cells. Further, the constriction of capillaries reduces the blood's ability to remove waste products. The result is an overall condition of stagnation and an accumulation of toxic excess that interferes with the flow of sensory impulses and energy. The result can be a diminished sensitivity to touch and other forms of stimulation.

In men, excessive consumption of foods high in saturated fat and cholesterol often leads to trouble in the prostate gland and to constriction and blockage of the blood vessels that supply the penis. These are leading causes of impotence. The first signs of trouble in the prostate are often small microscopic modules, known as prostatic concretions, that appear in the alkaline fluid secreted by the gland. If plenty of hard fats are consumed, especially the kinds of fats in cheese, butter, ice cream, and other dairy products, and if iced or chilled foods or drinks are taken in excess, the concretions may harden and calcify in a manner similar to the formation of kidney stones. Prostatic concretions may accumulate in the tissue of the gland in the form of cysts.

In many cases, these accumulations cause the prostate to enlarge. Enlargement is further aggravated by the intake of sugar, fruits, alcohol, honey, orange juice, ice cream, coffee, and drugs and medications, all of which have an extreme yin or expansive quality. Benign prostatic enlargement has become nearly universal among men: it is estimated that 10 percent of American men experience some form of enlargement by the age of forty and practically 100 percent experience it by the age of sixty. The condition of the prostate has a direct effect on male sexuality.

The prostate gland has a compact and tight structure and is located below the bladder. It surrounds the urethra, the tube that conveys sperm and urine to the outside via the penis. It also surrounds the ejaculatory ducts through which sperm and seminal fluid travel en route to the urethra. During sex, tightening and contraction of the prostate stimulates erection of the penis. At the moment of orgasm, the discharge of chakra energy causes the prostate to contract forcefully. A wave of contractions then spreads outward along the penis. If the prostate becomes enlarged, weakened, or filled with calcified cysts, its contracting power diminishes, interfering with the man's ability to generate or maintain erection and with the intensity of orgasm.

Overconsumption of saturated fat and cholesterol can diminish vaginal sensitivity and slow the secretion of vaginal lubrication. It is this fluid that provides the medium for the exchange of energy between the penis and the vagina, similar to the way that saliva acts as a medium for the breakdown and digestion of food in the mouth. This condition develops when a thin layer of hard fat accumulates just below the surface of the vaginal membrane. Fatty accumulations in these tissues can dull sensory nerve impulses and clog the minute passageways through which vaginal lubrication is secreted. A similar condition may develop in the labia and clitoris, making them less flexible and sensitive to touch. The conditions diminish a woman's sexual pleasure, sometimes to the point that orgasm becomes difficult to achieve.

The accumulation of hard fat also affects other organs in the female reproductive system. These accumulations may take the form of fibroid tumors, blockages in the Fallopian tubes, dermoid cysts, and in extreme cases, cancer of the ovaries, uterus, or cervix. These conditions interfere with female sexuality. Vaginal discharge is a common indication that excess is beginning to build up in the reproductive organs, and menstrual disorders also indicate this. An estimated 40 percent of women in America suffer from premenstrual syndrome (PMS), and 3 percent have severe cases. In addition, 40 percent of women have fibroid tumors. Surgeons annually perform over 4 million operations on female genital organs, including about 700,000 hysterectomies. Again, these gynecological disorders are largely the result of improper diet.

Breast cancer, which now affects one in ten American women, is being increasingly linked to a high-fat diet, especially the overconsumption of milk and other dairy products. In a study published in the February 15, 1989 issue of *Journal of the National Cancer Institute*, dairy food was found to be the most potent factor in the development of breast cancer. A study of 250 women with breast cancer in Vercelli, a province in northwestern Italy, found that they tended to consume considerably more milk, high-fat cheese, and butter than 499 healthy women of the same age. Another report in the August 15, 1989 issue of *Journal of the National Cancer Institute* found that a high-fat, low-fiber diet may increase the chances of getting breast cancer. Swedish scientists found that the typical modern diet was associated with tumor size, and that women with more favorable prognostic signs consumed more fiber, foods with vitamin A, and less fat.

Dairy consumption has also been linked with ovarian cancer by researchers at Harvard. In a report in the July 8, 1989 issue of *The Lancet,* a British medical journal, scientists noted that women with ovarian cancer had low blood levels of transferase, an enzyme involved in the metabolism of dairy foods. The researchers theorized that women with low levels of transferase who eat dairy foods, especially yogurt and cottage cheese, could increase their risk of ovarian cancer by as much as three times.

Overintake of saturated fat and cholesterol also lessens flexibility. As hard fat accumulates in the muscles, tissues, organs, and joints, they become harder and less elastic. Flexibility is a sign that energy is flowing smoothly throughout the body, while rigidity means that energy is blocked or stagnated. Children, for example, are usually softer and more flexible than adults, and the flow of energy through their bodies is less restricted. A healthy conductivity to environmental energy creates a higher rate of physical and mental activity, including a greater capacity for sexual enjoyment. Mental attributes such as creativity, open-mindedness, playfulness, honesty, and imagination also result from a flexible mind and body and enhance the enjoyment of sex.

As we can see, the way we eat affects not only our physical condition but also our outlook on sex. Animal foods stimulate the body to produce testosterone and other more yang hormones and suppress production of estrogen and other more yin hormones, except in cases where livestock have been fed artificial estrogens. An excess of male hormones can make people think and act more aggressively. In some cases, rather than being a loving exchange between partners, sex becomes like a sporting event with each partner competing for the best "performance." Sex may come to be equated with scoring points on the playing field. It may assume a predatory character with all of the rules of the hunt, or become like a military confrontation, with the goal being to achieve as many "conquests" as possible. The peaceful yet dynamic relationship between men and women can easily turn into the "battle of the sexes." When carried to extremes, this tendency can lead to the desire to dominate another person or to a preference for sadistic sexual practices.

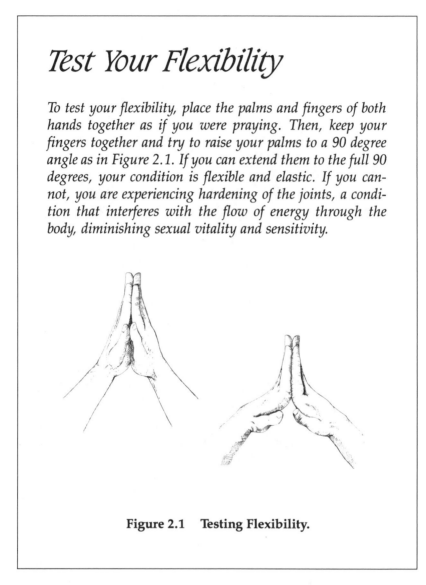

Test Your Flexibility

To test your flexibility, place the palms and fingers of both hands together as if you were praying. Then, keep your fingers together and try to raise your palms to a 90 degree angle as in Figure 2.1. If you can extend them to the full 90 degrees, your condition is flexible and elastic. If you cannot, you are experiencing hardening of the joints, a condition that interferes with the flow of energy through the body, diminishing sexual vitality and sensitivity.

Figure 2.1   Testing Flexibility.

THE ROLE OF STRESS

Stress has become a byword referring to all the pressure, tugs, pushes, and pulls to which people in modern society are subjected. It is often cited as interfering with the desire for, or enjoyment of, sex. Although external pressures contribute to stress, diet plays a major role in influencing how we respond to the challenges of living.

Meat, eggs, cheese, chicken, and other animal products produce tightness or tension in the body, reducing flexibility and restricting the flow of energy through the chakras, meridians, and cells of the body. In this condition, which we may refer to as "yang stress," we easily become tense and unable to relax. We may become too preoccupied with outside problems such as work, money, or time pressures to respond joyfully and creatively to sexual stimulation.

On the other hand, a diet high in sugar, soft drinks, chocolate, spices, tropical fruits, and other strong yin foods dissipates energy, often to the point that we feel unable to successfully manage day-to-day challenges, including those that revolve around sexuality and relationships. Often, these foods produce a sense that things are "out of control," together with a sense of being overwhelmed or weighed down by external events or pressures. This condition, which we may refer to as "yin stress," interferes with the energetic pursuit of sexuality.

When we are healthy, the difficulties and pressures of the outside world are seen as challenges that invigorate and energize us. The flexibility of our thinking is related to the flexibility of our bodies. Whether we respond to challenges in a creative way or whether we are overwhelmed by them is due largely to our state of health.

Eating well is the long-term answer to both types of stress. A moderately balanced diet of whole grains and vegetables produces a calming and centering effect on the body and mind, energizes vitality, and helps relax feelings of tension or pressure. We become more relaxed, centered, and in control, and better able to pursue and enjoy the pleasures of lovemaking.

THE CAUSE OF FATIGUE

Sexuality demands a certain amount of physical vitality and energy. Chronic fatigue, which for many people is a fact of life, interferes with our ability to generate chakra energy.

Hypoglycemia, or chronic low blood sugar, is a common

contributor to chronic fatigue. This condition is related to the health and functioning of the pancreas. The hard fats contained in animal foods, especially those in chicken, cheese, eggs, and shellfish, often accumulate in the pancreas, making the organ become hard and tight. The pancreas secretes the hormones insulin and anti-insulin (glucagon). Insulin keeps the blood sugar level down, while anti-insulin causes it to rise. These hormones are properly balanced in the healthy person, and the level of blood sugar stays within the normal range.

Insulin is a more yang hormone, while anti-insulin is more yin. Elevated blood sugar indicates a more yin condition, while low blood sugar means that the condition has become more yang. When blood sugar rises, insulin is automatically secreted in order to bring it down. If, for example, someone eats refined sugar, ice cream, fruit, chocolate, or other simple sugars that are more extreme yin, the level of sugar in the blood rises rapidly and insulin is secreted. Salty foods, concentrated animal fats, and proteins lower blood sugar, and when this happens the pancreas secretes anti-insulin in order to bring it up. If we are healthy, pancreatic hormones act to maintain the proper level of sugar in the blood.

However, when the pancreas becomes overly tight and hard fats develop within it, it is no longer able to secrete anti-insulin properly. The result is chronic low blood sugar, or hypoglycemia. This condition becomes especially acute in the afternoon or evening as the atmosphere becomes still and quiet. As the blood sugar level dips below normal, the person feels anxiety, depression, or fatigue, along with cravings for sugar or strong sweets. At this time, the person will seek a chocolate bar, soft drink, or coffee with sugar. In some cases, the condition is severe enough that they turn to alcohol or to drugs, which are even more extreme, in an attempt to make balance.

These extreme fluctuations in metabolism—the low of hypoglycemia followed by the rapid but short-lived burst of energy provided by eating refined or other simple sugars—have a direct effect on sexuality. Low blood sugar is often accompanied by chronic fatigue that interferes with the desire for sex and the ability to perform sexually. In some cases, one partner may be looking forward to sex, but if the other is suffering from hypoglycemia he or she may respond, "Not tonight, honey, I'm too tired," or "Not now . . . I'm not in the mood." Moreover, bouts of depression can also be triggered by low blood sugar. These bouts undermine self-confidence and can produce anxiety about sex and relationships.

Another long-term effect of consuming simple sugars is that they deplete the body's reserve of minerals, and with them our energy and vitality. In the normal digestive process, complex sugars such as those in whole grains, beans, and sweet-flavored vegetables are decomposed gradually and at an even rate by various enzymes in the mouth, stomach, pancreas, and intestines. Complex sugars enter the bloodstream slowly after being broken down into smaller saccharide units. During the process, the pH of the blood maintains a normally healthy, slightly alkaline quality.

By contrast, simple (single and double) sugars such as those of refined sugar, honey, and fruit are metabolized quickly, causing the blood to become overacidic. Refined sugar is an extremely alkaloid substance. When it enters the bloodstream an acid reaction takes place. Our life and health depend on maintaining a weak alkaline reaction in the bloodstream. Sickness and dysfunction results if the blood becomes too acid or too alkaline. To compensate for an overacidic condition, our chemical metabolism uses stored minerals, including calcium, for buffer reactions that are necessary to·maintain blood alkalinity. This process produces excessive carbon dioxide and water, elements that are normally discharged through breathing and urination. Moreover, the intake of refined sugar causes the pancreas to secrete insulin, which allows excess sugar in the blood to be removed and enter the cells of the body. This produces a burst of energy as the glucose (the end product of all sugar metabolism) is oxidized and carbon dioxide and water are given off as waste products.

Much of the sugar that enters the bloodstream is originally stored in the liver in the form of glycogen until needed, when it is again changed into glucose. When the amount of glycogen exceeds the liver's storage capacity of about fifty grams, it is released into the bloodstream in the form of fatty acid. This fatty acid is stored first in the more inactive places of the body

Body Scrubbing to Energize Sexual Vitality

Scrubbing your body with a moist, hot towel is a wonderfully natural way to relieve stress, relax tension, and energize your vitality. It takes only about ten minutes to do.

Body scrubbing can be done before or after a bath or shower, or anytime. All you need is a sink with hot water and a medium-sized cotton bath towel. Turn on the hot water. Hold the towel at either end and place the center of the towel under the stream of hot water. Wring out the towel, and while it is still hot and steamy begin to scrub with it. Do a section of the body at a time. For example, begin with the hands and fingers and work your way up the arms to the shoulders, neck, and face, then down to the chest, upper back, abdomen, lower back, buttocks, legs, feet, and toes. Scrub until the skin turns slightly red or until each part becomes warm. Reheat the towel by running it under hot water after doing each section or as soon as it starts to cool.

The body scrub releases blockage and allows environmental energy to flow more smoothly through the body. In the morning, atmospheric energy moves in an outward and upward direction, producing the tendency toward activity. In the evening, atmospheric energy moves downward and inward, producing the tendency toward relaxation and rest. Body scrubbing puts us more in touch with the natural coming and going, waxing and waning, upward and downward flow of energy in the atmosphere. A morning body scrub has the effect of activating energy flow and vitality. When done in the evening, a body scrub calms and relaxes us, melting and dissolving tension and stress. Moreover, scrubbing with a hot towel helps melt deposits of hard fat just below the skin, increasing its sensitivity to touch and energizing the flow of energy along the meridians.

such as the buttocks, breasts, thighs, and midsection. Then, if cane sugar, fruit sugar, dairy sugar, and other simple sugars are eaten excessively, fatty acid continues to build up, this time in organs such as the heart, liver, kidneys, ovaries, and prostate gland, which gradually become filled with fatty mucus.

As these accumulations penetrate the inner tissues, the normal functioning of these organs begins to weaken. The flow of energy along the primary channel and in the chakras is also diminished. The person often begins to experience chronic fatigue and lack of vitality and a diminished desire for sex. In extreme cases, the buildup of fat can lead to blockage—as in atherosclerosis—or to the formation of cysts, tumors, and eventually cancer. The female breasts and organs in the reproductive tract are especially sensitive to these accumulations.

The modern habit of consuming icy cold foods and drinks, which are extreme yin, also influences sexuality. These items weaken the ability to generate chakra energy and make a person cold. The energy generated by the chakras can be thought of as a form of heat. The chakras are in fact referred to as "energy furnaces."

Before the modern age, people were often wary of consuming iced foods or beverages, even in hot weather. Hippocrates, for example, stated in his *Regimen:* "Why should anyone run the hazard in the heat of summer of drinking iced waters, which are excessively cold, and suddenly throwing the body into a different state from the one it was in before, producing thereby many ill effects?" When we eat ice cream or drink an iced beverage, the body reacts to the shock of extreme cold by raising the body temperature. Additional energy must be generated to compensate, and if this practice continues, the body's energy reserves may become depleted. The result is chronic fatigue, lack of vitality, and a weakening of sexual charge. Many people experience a lessening of sexual vitality during the heat of summer. The consumption of iced foods and beverages, which tends to increase during the heat, is a major cause of this.

As we can see, our diet has a profound effect on our sexuality. Daily food is a decisive factor in our sexual lives. What takes place in the kitchen often determines what happens in the bedroom.

FOODS THAT ENHANCE SEXUALITY

The energy of whole natural foods such as whole cereal grains, beans, fresh local vegetables, sea vegetables, and others is more centrally balanced than that of the extreme foods described above. These foods are neither too yin nor too yang and have the effect of harmonizing sexual energy. The complex carbohydrates in whole grains, beans, and fresh local vegetables have a number of advantages in helping to promote sexual harmony. Because they are slowly broken down and absorbed into the bloodstream, they provide a slow, steady supply of energy. This contributes to endurance and staying power.

A second advantage comes from the binding power of complex carbohydrates. They are made up of many smaller sugar molecules bound together, and exist naturally along with minerals, proteins, fats, and fiber. Eating them promotes the physical endurance needed for sex. By contrast, simple sugars have a fragmented structure and are made up of many loose molecules of single or double sugars. They are dominated by a more yin or expanding force. When we eat them, we receive a quick burst of energy that is short lived. Alcohol, another form of simple sugar, has a similar effect. Being yin, it initially melts tightness in the body and loosens inhibitions. When consumed excessively, however, it makes sexual potency more difficult to achieve.

Hundreds of thousands of people throughout the world have begun to include more balanced natural foods in their diets. Many have experienced a return of sexual vitality and have discovered the joy of satisfying relationships following a change in diet. This overall dietary pattern, based on the dynamic balance between yin and yang, is known today as "macrobiotics."

An optimal diet for healthy sexuality is one that avoids heavy saturated fats, refined sugars, tropical fruits and vegetables, and other foods that either block or weaken the flow of energy along the primary channel and in the chakras. In a temperate climate, complex carbohydrates should comprise the mainstay of the diet. These include the complex carbohydrates in whole cereal grains, beans and bean products, fresh local vegetables, and sea vegetables. Vegetable sources of protein—which contain no saturated fat and cholesterol—are preferred over animal sources. Proper mineral balance, provided from such natural seasonings as sea salt, which contains many trace minerals, and sea vegetables, strengthens vitality and endurance and increases the sensitivity of the nervous system. In general, minerals provide the drive; protein and fat, the substance; and carbohydrates, the energy for sex. For healthy and satisfying sex, it is essential that these elements be of the highest quality.

See Figure 2.2 for the daily proportions of foods that are recommended for optimal health, including the enjoyment of sexuality.

Whole Cereal Grains

Whole cereal grains are the seed of new life. Grains are formed through the union of oppositely charged male and female energies within the cereal plant. When placed in the soil, they sprout and grow into a new generation of plants.

In human myth and custom, cereal grains are associated with fertility and abundance. As Margaret Visser states in *Much Depends on Dinner,*

> Everywhere rice is a symbol of fecundity. In Hindu marriage ceremonies the couple have to stand in a shallow basket while rice is poured over their heads. In our own society, a long way outside the area where rice reigns, the . . . grains are traditionally flung at newly wed couples as they leave church. A great length of time and many happy events are imagined by the guests throwing rice, in addition to fertility.

Whole grains such as brown rice, barley, millet, oats, corn, rye, wheat, and buckwheat can comprise up to 50 to 60 percent of daily consumption. They contain an ideal proportion of min-

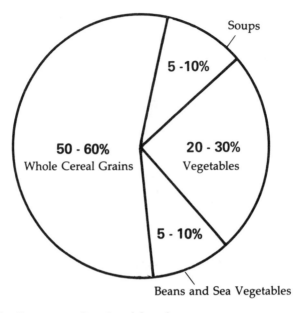

Plus Beverages, Occasional Supplementary
Foods, Seasonings, and Condiments

Figure 2.2   General Proportions of the Macrobiotic Diet.

erals, protein, carbohydrates, and vitamins, and when absorbed by the body release energy at a slow, steady rate. Refined or polished grains lack this balance and are therefore not
recommended for regular consumption. This gradual, peaceful
release makes it easier to sustain and control the buildup of
energy during intercourse.

The ideal way to eat grains is in their whole form rather than
in the form of flour, although some flour products, including
whole grain noodles and unyeasted whole grain breads, are
fine on occasion. However, overintake of bread, muffins, pan-
cakes, crackers, and other baked flour products can produce
stagnation in the digestive tract and interfere with the smooth
flow of energy along the primary channel, especially in the
stomach and hara chakras.

Whole grains are also an excellent source of fiber. The intake
of fiber, especially that in whole grains, promotes the smooth

function of the intestinal tract, which in turn permits energy to flow smoothly in the lower body, including in the hara and sexual chakras. On the other hand, the modern diet, which is very low in fiber and high in fats (often in the form of oily, sticky, and greasy foods) and simple sugars, can cause energy in the intestines and lower body to stagnate. In this condition it is much more difficult to generate the energy needed for sex.

Each grain has a slightly different effect on sexual response. Grains that grow in colder climates are more yang. They have a tough, fibrous outer coat and are often crushed into flour before being eaten. Grains that come from warmer, sunnier climates are more yin, as are those that are softer and have a more delicate consistency. Buckwheat, for example, was a traditional staple in Russia and other cold northern areas, while corn is grown more in warm sunny places including Central and South America. More yang, hardy grains such as buckwheat, rye, wheat, and millet, tend to activate the lower chakras and energize our physical vitality. More yin grains such as barley and corn activate upward energy and heighten our emotional responses. Brown rice, which is centrally balanced in terms of expanding and contracting energies, especially charges the hara and midbrain chakras and harmonizes the physical aspects of love and sex with the emotional and spiritual aspects.

Soups

Soups are a good source of energy and nutrients, especially when made with high-quality natural ingredients. Fresh local vegetables, sea vegetables such as wakame and kombu, whole grains, and beans are fine for regular use in soup. Traditionally prepared, naturally processed seasonings such as miso and tamari soy sauce are especially good used as flavorings for soups. Ideally, soups should be made every day from fresh natural ingredients, and not eaten from a can or package. One or two small bowls of soup are fine for daily consumption.

Traditional miso soup, made from all natural ingredients, is especially helpful in establishing flexibility and restoring the smooth flow of energy throughout the body. Traditional Oriental doctors long ago valued miso and other fermented soybean foods for their properties in helping the body discharge fats and other toxic substances. Miso soup helps prevent the buildup of these substances in the body and contributes to the strength and elasticity of the circulatory system and body as a whole, thus enhancing our ability to appreciate the many dimensions of love and sexuality. As discussed in the book *Macrobiotic Diet* (Japan Publications), in the 1960s medical researchers for the Japanese government began a long-term study of miso soup consumption and its effects on the nation's health. The dietary habits, incidence of degenerative disease, and mortality rates of 265,000 men and women over forty years old were studied over a twelve-year period. In 1982, the National Cancer Center Research Institute released its final study showing that those who never ate miso soup had a 43 percent higher death rate from coronary heart disease and a 33 percent higher death rate from stomach cancer than those who consumed miso soup daily. Those who did not eat miso also had 29 percent more fatal strokes, 3.5 times more deaths resulting from high blood pressure, and 19 percent more cancer at all sites in the body. Moreover, miso and tamari soy sauce contain beneficial enzymes and bacteria that strengthen the intestines, thereby energizing and vitalizing the flow of energy in the hara and sexual chakras.

Vegetables

A wide selection of fresh vegetables can be eaten daily. They may comprise between 25 and 30 percent of daily intake. Organically grown varieties are preferred, since fertilizers, insecticides, and other chemicals used in modern agriculture can diminish sexual vitality. Moreover, irradiated vegetables, which are sold in many food stores, are also potentially damaging to sexuality and reproductive ability. Being extremely yin, radiation produces chemical changes in foods that cause them to become more yin. Their life energy is weakened, and as a result, bacteria cannot grow in them. Eating them causes us to become weaker as well.

Green cabbage, kale, broccoli, cauliflower, collards, pumpkin, watercress, Chinese cabbage, bok choy, dandelion, mustard greens, daikon greens, scallion, onions, daikon, turnips, acorn squash, butternut squash, buttercup squash, burdock, carrots, and other seasonally available varieties are fine for regular use.

For optimal vitality, it is better to cook the majority of your vegetable dishes. They can be sautéed with a small amount of high-quality, naturally processed oil such as sesame or corn; steamed; boiled; and sometimes prepared using tamari soy sauce or light sea salt as seasoning. Pickled vegetables without spices may also be used daily in small volume.

Each of the major categories of vegetables—for example, root, round, and leafy—influences the body's energy flow, and hence sexuality, in a slightly different way. Vegetables such as daikon, carrots, or turnips, which contain both a root and leafy green portion, can help us understand these effects more clearly.

The leafy green portion of a vegetable contains strong upward energy that charges and vitalizes the upper body and chakras. Including leafy greens in the daily diet stimulates the functions produced by these chakras, especially our sensitivity to more subtle forms of touch and other stimulation. They help make our expression become more refined and sensitive.

The root portion of a vegetable is strongly charged with downward energy that activates the lower chakras, including those in the hara and sexual chakras. Eating these vegetables energizes us physically. Kinpira, a traditional dish served in many macrobiotic households, is often eaten to vitalize energy and reduce fatigue. This dish can be made with carrots and burdock. Burdock is a long brown root vegetable that grows wild in many parts of North America. Moreover, jinenjo, or Japanese mountain potato (a different species than common potato), was used in Far Eastern cooking to activate physical and sexual vitality.

Round vegetables, including fall or winter squashes, cabbage, and onions, contain a more even balance of expanding and contracting energy. They activate the middle regions of the body, including the heart and stomach chakras. Since they are good sources of complex carbohydrates, eating them helps to stabilize the level of sugar in the blood and, because they influence the heart chakra, contributes to a deepening of emotional sensitivity and responsiveness.

When selecting vegetables, it is important to choose those that are grown or that have originated in a climate similar to the one in which we live. Vegetables that originated in the tropics, including tomatoes, potatoes, eggplant, and others, contribute to a dimineralization in the body that weakens sexual vitality in the long run. They are extremely yin or expansive and cause chakra energy to become dispersed or weak. Among tropical vegetables, avocados contain very strong upward energy that is especially weakening to sexual potency. The vegetables of the nightshade family (such as tomatoes, eggplant, and potatoes) have also been linked to arthritis, or, in other words, calcification and stiffening of the joints. This condition diminishes flexibility and capacity to initiate or respond to sexual stimulation. Therefore, vegetables in the nightshade family or those high in oxalic acid, simple sugar, fat, or potassium (all very yin), such as potatoes (including sweet potatoes and yams), tomatoes, eggplant, peppers, asparagus, spinach, beets, zucchini, and avocado, are best avoided for regular use. Mayonnaise and other high-fat or oily dressings are also best avoided.

Cooking vegetables and other foods contributes to their energizing effect on the chakras and on sexuality. Aside from being more difficult to digest, raw vegetables have a cooling or chilling effect on the body. When eaten excessively, they diminish the body's ability to generate energy, and they weaken sexual vitality. The more yin, expanding, and cooling effects of raw vegetables and fruits are used in the modern diet to balance the contractive, heat-producing effects of meat, eggs, cheese, poultry, and other forms of animal food. The rising popularity of raw salads is a result of the steady increase in consumption of beef, chicken, cheese, and other animal foods that has occurred in modern times.

In the order of the universe, yin attracts yang, and yang attracts yin. The more we consume foods with strong contracting energy, the more we seek foods with strong expanding energy to make balance.

This balancing principle helps explain why tomatoes, green peppers, potatoes, various spicy herbs, chocolate, coffee, and other foods from the tropics have become increasingly popular in modern diets. These foods are far more expansive than those originating in temperate climates, and help to neutralize or balance the strong contractive energy in meat and other animal foods. However, this balance is based on extremes and leads to imbalance in the body, including problems with sexual health.

Moreover, the modern diet relies heavily on intensive cooking methods that employ high heat including grilling, charcoal broiling, and deep frying. These energy-intensive methods also create the desire for fresh, cooling foods such as raw salads and fruits (including tropical varieties), as well as for chilled foods and drinks. This extreme dietary pattern disrupts the normal balance of energy in the body and creates the extreme tendencies in health and behavior that are so common today.

Beans and Sea Vegetables

When eaten with whole grains, beans make a complete protein and provide all the amino acids needed by the body. The most suitable varieties for regular use are low-fat azuki beans, chickpeas, black soybeans, and lentils. Other beans are fine for use on occasion. Bean products such as tofu, tempeh, and natto can be used.

The complex carbohydrates in beans and foods derived from beans provide a slow, steady source of energy midway between the quick, rapid energy created by most vegetables and the calm, peaceful strength provided by whole grains. Beans and bean products are also very high in calcium and have been studied for their ability to restore health and elasticity to the circulatory system. As a part of a balanced whole foods diet, beans and bean products such as tofu, tempeh, miso, and tamari soy sauce contribute to smooth functioning of chakra

Sweet Vegetable Drink

Sweet vegetables provide a readily available source of complex carbohydrates that can help relieve the symptoms of hypoglycemia, including fatigue, anxiety, the craving for sweets, and a diminished appetite for sex. They may be eaten regularly in the diet, or taken in the more concentrated form of sweet vegetable drink. To prepare this special drink, cut equal amounts of carrots, squash (select those with an orange color on the inside), onions, and green cabbage into very fine pieces. Place the cut vegetables in a pot with four times as much water, cover, and bring to a boil. Reduce the flame to low and simmer for 15–20 minutes. Remove from the stove and strain the liquid through a fine mesh strainer into a large glass jar. The leftover vegetable chunks can be used in soups, stews, or other dishes.

The strained liquid—or "sweet vegetable drink"—can be stored in the refrigerator for several days. One or two cups can be taken daily or several times per week depending on the severity of the condition. Sweet vegetable drink may be continued for a month or so or until the symptoms of hypoglycemia improve. To serve, heat in a saucepan until warm, or allow it to set for several minutes until it becomes room temperature.

energy and the overall health of the digestive, circulatory, and nervous systems.

Beans, and azuki beans in particular, have a vitalizing and strengthening effect on the kidneys, adrenal glands, and sexual organs. The healthy functioning of these organs and glands is essential for sexual and reproductive vitality. Soybeans, which are higher in protein and fat than many other varieties of beans, have been found to benefit the condition of the blood vessels and circulatory system. However, in the case of soybean foods, we need to consider the way in which the beans were processed in order to understand how they affect sexuality. Soybean milk or curd is generally the most yin part of the bean. Tofu, which is made from soy milk, is also very yin or expansive. It generally has a cooling effect on the body, and if eaten excessively—especially raw—can diminish sexual desire. The same is true of soy milk, soy ice cream, and desserts made by combining tofu—already more yin—with fruit or natural sweeteners. For sexual vitality, it is better to minimize the intake of these foods and to cook tofu and season it mildly with tamari soy sauce, miso, or another traditional seasoning that has a slightly salty flavor.

Coastal societies, including those in the Far East, have long recognized the importance of sea vegetables in contributing to the flexibility of body and mind. In Oriental medicine, sea vegetables were identified with strengthening the blood, the heart, and the circulatory system. They are also excellent for the kidneys, the urinary system, and the sexual organs. They give elasticity to arteries, veins, and organ tissues, contributing to flexibility and the smooth flow of chakra energy.

Varieties such as nori, wakame, kombu, hijiki, arame, dulse, and agar-agar can be used daily or often. Sea vegetables are a rich source of minerals and help strengthen the nervous system, enhancing sensitivity to more subtle forms of stimulation. The minerals in sea vegetables also conduct electromagnetic energy from the environment and increase the conductivity of the chakras and meridians to this energy. Sea vegetables were also used for centuries in the Far East as natural beauty aids; they were valued for their properties of promoting beautiful, shiny hair and soft, smooth skin.

In general, beans, bean products, and sea vegetables may comprise up to 10 percent of the daily diet.

Occasional Foods

Among animal foods, those lowest in fat are preferred for occasional consumption. In temperate climates, low-fat, white-meat fish is preferred and can be eaten one to three times a week, depending on each person's condition and needs. Meat, poultry, eggs, cheese, and other dairy products are best avoided for maximum health and enjoyment of sexuality.

Fruits may also be eaten on occasion as a part of a balanced whole foods diet. However, compared with whole grains, beans, and vegetables from land and sea, fruits contain much smaller amounts of complex carbohydrates, fiber, protein, un-saturated fat, and essential vitamins and minerals. Most of their composition is water. Fructose, the primary carbohydrate in fruit, is a simple sugar and enters the bloodstream more rapidly than the complex carbohydrates found in grains and vegetables. Moreover, the energy fruits give is very cooling, light, and expansive and needs to be balanced by the strong centering energy of cooked whole grains, beans, vegetables, and the other foods mentioned above.

Taken in excess, fruits—especially tropical and semitropical varieties—can deplete chakra energy and weaken sexual vital-ity. They produce a cooling or chilling effect on the body and can make it more difficult to generate heat and chakra energy during sex. In general, fruits can be eaten three or four times per week as a part of a balanced natural foods diet. Temperate varieties such as apples, pears, peaches, melons, and berries are preferred for regular use. For maximum energy and vitality, tropical fruits such as bananas, papayas, and mangoes are best avoided by those living in the temperate regions. The strong yin energy of fruit can be somewhat balanced by cooking them with a pinch of natural sea salt, or by drying them. Raw fruits have the strongest expansive or dispersing effects on chakra energy and sexual vitality.

A variety of natural snacks may also be enjoyed from time to time, including lightly roasted seeds such as sesame, pump-kin, and sunflower. Nuts may also be consumed from time to time, but intake of tropical varieties, which are oily and fatty, is best minimized. Natural snacks such as rice cakes, puffed whole grain cereals, and popcorn (without butter) are also fine. Leftover whole grains and other dishes can also be eaten as snacks.

Seasonings and Condiments

High-quality natural seasonings such as sea salt, miso, and tamari soy sauce can be used regularly. However, care must be taken not to overuse salty seasonings. Salt, which has strong contracting energy, can make the chakras and body as a whole more tight and less conductive to energy. All spices are extremely expansive and have the opposite effect on sexuality. Taken in combination with meat and other animal foods, they can sometimes trigger the uncontrollable release of stored yang energy. This can lead to emotional outbursts or instability, and in extreme cases, to so-called "crimes of passion." Alcohol, which is also strongly yin, has a similar effect. Spices, including mustard, pepper, and curry, sometimes act to temporarily stimulate sexual arousal. However, these effects are short term. Because of their strong yin effects, spices weaken sexual vitality and potency, especially when eaten as a part of a vegetarian or semi-vegetarian diet.

For optimal health and flexibility, quality vegetable oils are preferred, especially unrefined sesame or corn oil. Natural sweeteners, especially those derived from complex carbohydrate sources such as rice or barley, are better than honey, maple syrup, fructose, or refined sugar. High-quality natural rice syrup or barley malt can be used from time to time to add a sweet flavor to desserts and other dishes.

A variety of natural, nonspicy table condiments can be used to enhance the flavor and nutritional value of daily foods. Gomashio, or "sesame salt," made from combining roasted sesame seeds with sea salt (see recipe on page 173), helps to energize sexual vitality. The minerals in sea salt contribute to the strength and vitality of the circulatory system and other body functions, while the natural oils in sesame seeds enhance flexibility. Other condiments, including sea vegetable powders, umeboshi (naturally pickled plums), naturally fermented brown rice, and umeboshi vinegars, are also fine for regular use in moderate amounts. As previously mentioned, spicy condiments, including mustard, pepper, catsup, and others, are best avoided for optimal vitality and health.

Beverages

Coffee, commercial tea, and most herbal teas are strongly charged with yin or upward energy. When taken in excess, they stimulate mental activity at the expense of physical and sexual vitality. Nonaromatic and nonstimulant beverages are preferred for regular use. Traditional beverages such as bancha twig tea, cereal grain teas and coffees, and other nonstimulant, nonaromatic varieties are fine for regular use. The sweet vegetable drink described on page 44 can also be used on a regular basis. Soft drinks, tropical fruit juices, and strong alcoholic drinks are best avoided.

THE ENERGY OF COOKING

When we cook, we rebalance the energy and quality of food. The quality of energy supplied during cooking directly influences the way in which our daily foods effect our physical, mental, and emotional condition, including our sexuality.

Cooking methods that are quick and light, such as quick steaming or boiling, activate upward energy in the body. These methods are often used when cooking leafy greens and other vegetables. Dishes such as quickly steamed or blanched greens and other vegetables activate the upper chakras and enhance the ability to respond to more subtle forms of stimulation.

Dishes that are cooked for longer periods, usually over a low flame, such as vegetable or grain soups or stews, or pressure-cooked or boiled grains, beans, and other foods, have the effect of concentrating energy. They contribute to the basic drive or vitality needed for sexual attraction and activity.

In general, more peaceful, natural methods of cooking are preferred for harmonious sexual relations. Extreme or artificial methods of cooking disrupt the natural flow of energy in the body. Baking, for example, although fine for occasional use by those in good health, is a very concentrated or yang method of cooking. When grains are baked, they are first crushed into flour. This fragments and disperses their energy. Then water is added to make dough, along with some type of fermenting agent, further adding to the expansive quality of the flour. However, the dough is then placed in an enclosed oven and baked at high temperatures until it rises and hardens. Concentrated heat causes the flour to become hard and dry. The effect of eating too many baked flour products—especially cookies, crackers, and muffins—is to constrict the chakras and make it more difficult to generate sexual energy. This tightening or hardening effect can also involve the joints and internal organs and is especially prevalent in the middle and lower body, including the stomach and hara chakras. One result is a tightening or hardening in the pancreas that can inhibit the ability of the organ to secrete glucagon (anti-insulin). This condition contributes to chronic low blood sugar and to the fatigue and lack of sexual vitality that often accompanies it.

As we saw earlier, modern energy-intensive methods of cooking, such as grilling and deep frying, produce chaotic effects on chakra and sexual energy. Being extreme, they create a desire for foods or drinks with the opposite, or extreme, cooling effects on the body. This extreme pattern scatters and weakens sexual energy. Artificial sources of heat, such as electric or microwave cooking, also disperse and weaken vitality.

Among modern cooking methods, gas cooking provides a flame that is responsive and easy to control and is preferred for optimal health and vitality. The proper use of fire or flame in cooking energizes and vitalizes the chakras and life energy as a whole. It increases our sensitivity and our ability to respond sexually.

The health hazards of electromagnetic fields can no longer be ruled out, according to a three-part series of articles published in *The New Yorker* in the summer of 1989. In addition to high voltage power lines, TVs, computers, and other electronic equipment, common household appliances such as vacuum cleaners, toasters, blenders, and fluorescent lights can be harmful to health. Electromagnetic fields are also generated by electric stoves. For cooking, most natural food cooks prefer to use a natural gas flame rather than electricity. It is very hard to fine tune cooking with electricity. It is a conductive heat that first warms the coils and then the pot and its contents from the bottom up. The temperature cannot be changed quickly when the control is turned to high or low because it takes some time to cool or heat the pot. Electricity makes it difficult to cook uniformly, and it is possible that the foods in the bottom of the pan can burn while those at the top are unfinished. A gas flame heats the surrounding air. Food thus cooks much more evenly, and the temperature can be adjusted immediately—a pot of water will instantly stop boiling when the flame is turned off, for example. Interestingly, many people who have shifted from electricity to gas have noticed immediate improvements in their energy levels and enjoyment of food.

Healthy sexuality depends upon a harmonious balance between expansion and contraction, or yin and yang, in our diets and in all aspects of daily living. Giving and receiving and initiating and responding are involved in the dynamics of love and sex, as are vitality and sensitivity. It is important, therefore, when selecting an optimal diet for sexuality, that both dimensions of energy be considered and well balanced. Sexuality involves the interplay of energy on many different levels. The foods we select and the methods we use to cook them need to reflect this diversity and provide a wide range of energies, tastes, and stimulation. In this way, we can come to appreciate sexuality in its fullest dimensions.

3.

Massage for Couples

Massage is a wonderful way for couples to communicate and help each other. It is one of the most important elements of Eastern and Western healing. Like acupuncture, it involves stimulating and unblocking the meridians and points along which electromagnetic energy, or *Ki*, flows throughout the body. As we have seen, energy flow becomes blocked or stagnated through accumulation of mucus, fats, or toxins in the blood, organs, or joints, which in turn causes stiffness or pain along the meridians. It is these blockages that interfere with a person's ability to respond sexually.

Basic massage (known in Japan as *Shiatsu*) uses only the hands and fingertips and can be learned in several hours. With practice, each partner can develop his or her ability and make massage into a comprehensive and effective healing art. It can help couples become closer to one another and can be done almost anytime and anywhere.

The style of massage presented in this chapter is based on a deep understanding of the energy constitution of the body and the interconnectedness of all of its parts and functions. Shiatsu is not an erotic or sexually arousing massage. Rather, it deals with underlying energy imbalances and helps improve overall vitality and conductivity to the forces of heaven and earth. In this way, it helps to activate sexual vitality and improve sensitivity.

Making your energy harmonious with that of your partner is an intrinsic element of massage, as it is in satisfying sex. It is therefore important to remember that the physical condition of both partners factor in its success. Someone who is healthy, eats a diet of whole grains and vegetables, and radiates a calm and vibrant energy will transfer this to their partner.

Keep in mind that the accumulation of mucus, fat, and other forms of excess and the resultant stagnation of energy in the chakras and meridians is caused largely by an imbalanced diet, especially overconsumption of saturated fats, dairy products, refined flour, sugar, fruits, and liquids. Therefore, along with massage, dietary adjustment is essential in establishing a smooth and active energy flow. Whole cereal grains, beans, fresh local vegetables, sea vegetables, and fermented soyfoods like miso and tamari soy sauce form the foundation of a healthful diet. When you eat right, your body eventually becomes clear and healthy so that massage can then be used for occasional recharging of one's already vibrant energy.

The basic full-body massage can be broken down into five stages:

1.   The shoulders, neck, and head.
2.   The back.
3.   The arms and hands.
4.   The legs and feet.
5.   The front of the body.

The basic massage routine presented on the following pages is flexible and can be adapted to each person's needs and condition. If, for example, a person is experiencing pain or severe rigidity in the joints or in any other part of the body, it is advisable to omit the procedures that call for massaging these areas. You can try the full-body massage one step at a time, or you can try only parts of it.

Also, unlike many other forms of massage, Shiatsu does not require the removal of clothing or the use of oils. Loose-fitting cotton clothing is best for giving and receiving massage. The massage can also be performed simply on blankets or cushions placed on the floor.

PART ONE: THE SHOULDERS, NECK, AND HEAD

Shoulders

If the shoulders are tight, swollen, and painful when pressed, energy is not flowing smoothly through the body. A person in this condition often has difficulty relaxing and may often be too tired to enjoy sex. These are also signs of stagnation in the intestines that blocks the active flow of energy to the sexual chakra and organs, diminishing their vitality and responsiveness.

To help relieve shoulder tension, release intestinal stagnation, and vitalize the flow of energy in the body as a whole, do the following.

1. Have your partner sit comfortably with his or her spine straight and shoulders and arms relaxed. Keeping your spine straight, kneel behind your partner. Extend your arms forward and grasp both shoulders with a firm but gentle pressure. (See Figure 3.1.) Keep your hands in this position and begin to harmonize your energies by breathing together. This will help your partner relax and make him or her more receptive to the massage. With your hands in this position, breathe together for about a minute.

2. Begin to massage the shoulders with a kneading motion. Start with the area closest to the neck and gradually work outward toward the tips of the shoulders. Repeat several times.

3. Stand up behind your partner. Keeping your thumbs straight, press with the tips of both thumbs along the top of the shoulder muscles on both sides of the neck. Gently push in and then quickly release the pressure. Begin from the innermost region on both sides of the neck, and work outward toward the tips of the shoulders.

    When performing this part of the massage, coordinate your breathing with that of your partner. To do this properly, inhale together, and as you breathe out, press down-

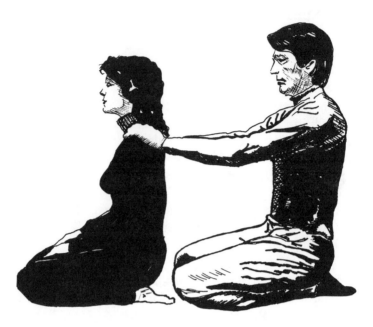

Figure 3.1   Preparing for Massage.

ward. Press along the shoulder muscle several times before proceeding to the next step of the massage.

4.   With your hands in the position indicated in step one,
     extend your middle fingers down the front of the body to
     massage the area under the collarbone on both sides. Us-
     ing the tips of the fingers, massage for about one minute.
     If this area is painful or overly sensitive, the lungs are
     overexpanded from mucus deposits, liquids, and sugar.

5.   Keeping your wrists loose and flexible, use the outside
     edge of your hands to gently pound the shoulders by
     rapidly alternating between the left and right hand. Begin
     at the neck and work your way outward. The shoulders
     can be done separately or both at the same time. Repeat
     several times.

     After finishing step five, again massage the shoulders as
     in step two.

Neck

Tension or stiffness in the neck is a common problem today, aggravated by the overconsumption of protein, saturated fat, sugar, refined foods, and overeating and overdrinking in general.

When the neck becomes stiff, energy does not flow smoothly through the small intestine, large intestine, stomach, bladder, and gall bladder meridians, all of which run along the neck. Stiffness in the neck also indicates diminished physical and mental flexibility, including a reduced capacity for sexual expression and enjoyment.

To relieve tension in the neck and stimulate the flow of energy to the organs and along these meridians, do the following.

1. Shift your position so that you are sitting behind your partner at a 45° angle. Place the bulk of your weight on one knee and raise your other leg so that your foot is on the floor, as shown in Figure 3.2. If you are right-handed, shift to the left so that you can use your left hand to support your partner's forehead, while leaving your right hand free to massage the back of the neck. Persons who are left-handed should shift in the opposite direction, leaving the left hand free for the neck massage.

2. Tilt your partner's head slightly backward and place the tips of your thumb and middle finger in the indented places at the base of the skull on both sides of the back of the neck. Massage this region for about a minute or until hardness or tension is relieved. Pain in this area frequently indicates an overconsumption of fatty foods, which interfere with the smooth functioning of the liver and gallbladder.

3. Return your partner's head to the normal angle and, beginning from the above regions, use the tip of your thumb and middle finger to massage in a straight line down the back of the neck to the base. Use a deep but gentle pinching motion in which you knead and stimulate the neck

Figure 3.2   Preparing Position for Neck Massage.

muscle with your fingertips. Repeat several times, making
sure to loosen any hardness or tension.

4.   Place the tip of your thumb in the center of the neck at the
     base of the skull. Begin breathing together, and after sev-
     eral breaths, tilt the head back, as in step two, and on the
     final inhalation, push your thumb inward and upward
     into the point, lifting the head slightly upward. Use your
     supporting hand to help lift the head. At the peak of the
     in-breath, vibrate your thumb for several seconds, and as
     you breathe out, release the pressure and allow the head
     to return to its normal position. Repeat several times.

5.   Return to your original position behind your partner. Place
     your right hand firmly on the shoulder, resting the inside
     of the hand against the neck for support. With your left
     hand on the left side of the head, begin to rotate the head
     slowly toward the right in a clockwise direction. This helps
     relax tension in the neck and shoulders. As much as possi-
     ble, allow the head to rotate itself; it is better to use your

hands only to support and guide the rotation. After a minute, reverse your hands and begin to rotate in the opposite, counterclockwise direction. This helps to stabilize the flow of energy in your partner's body. Continue for about one minute.

Head

In the human body and throughout nature, the part reflects the whole. This is especially true in the relationship between the head and the rest of the body, since there are areas on the head that relate to all of the major organs and body functions, including the chakras and sexual organs.

To stimulate these areas and their corresponding organs and functions, and to energize the body as a whole, do the following.

1. Stand up behind your partner. Place your fingers on either side of his or her head and extend your thumbs so that they are free to massage the central part of the top of the head. Place your thumbs behind each other and press down in a straight line extending from the hairline back across the top of the head and down the back of the head to the base of the skull. Repeat several times.

2. Directly on the top of the head in the center is a point known in Oriental countries as the "100 meeting point." Energy from all over the body gathers there. Place your fingers on either side of the receiver's head and position your thumbs just above the point. Breathe together several times, and at the peak of the final outbreath, press the 100 meeting point. While applying pressure, vibrate your thumbs for several seconds and then release. This helps to release energy that has become stagnant anywhere in the body. Repeat several times.

3. Referring to Figure 3.3, locate your partner's hair spiral. Position your hands as in step two, breathe together, and press your thumbs into the center of the spiral, using the same methods as above. Release and repeat several times.

The hair spiral is the place where heaven's force enters the body and from here flows down along the primary channel. Massaging the hair spiral helps to energize and vitalize the flow of energy in the chakras and the body as a whole.

4.   Extend your fingers down the sides of the head, and with your middle fingers massage both temples simultaneously using a slow, upward circular motion. Continue for about a minute or until all tension in this area is released.

5.   Grasp both ears with thumbs and middle fingers. Begin to massage the ears by pulling them gently upward from the top, outward from the side, and then downward from the lobe. Repeat several times, allowing your fingers to slide across the inner portion of the ear to the edge. The ears correlate with the kidneys, and this part of the massage is very good for loosening stagnation in these organs and improving sexual vitality.

6.   Using your fingertips, gently pound the top of the head,

Figure 3.3   Locating the Hair Spiral.

making sure to keep your wrists loose and flexible. You can also tighten your hands into a fist and gently pound the head with your knuckles. Be sure to stimulate the entire head, including the top, sides, and back. Do each region for about thirty seconds.

After finishing this part of the massage, sit down behind your partner and again knead the shoulders as explained previously. If the massage has been done properly, the shoulders should be softer and more relaxed, meaning that the flow of energy along the primary channel, chakras, and meridians is now smooth and active.

PART TWO: THE BACK

Massaging the back stimulates the flow of energy through all of the major organs. This is accomplished by massaging the bladder meridian (running along either side of the spine), the chakras, and the roots of the autonomic nerve branches (radiating outward from the spinal cord to the internal organs). The bladder meridian includes points where energy from the atmosphere enters the body and charges each of the major organs. To energize these organs and functions, do the following.

1. Have your partner lie on his or her stomach, the head turned sideways and arms extended comfortably to the side.

2. Kneel alongside your partner so that one hand is free to massage the entire back. If you are right-handed, sit on their left; vice versa if you are left-handed. Place your hand so that the center of the palm rests lightly on the spine. Slowly brush down the spine to the buttocks, as if you were smoothing the flow of energy downward.

3. Place one palm on the spine and place your other hand on top, as shown in Figure 3.4. Starting at the upper spine, breathe together, and as you exhale gently press downward. Add your body weight by leaning forward as you press. Release pressure during the next inhalation and repeat down the length of the spine to the tailbone.

Figure 3.4   Step Three of the Back Massage.

4. To massage the meridian running along the center of the
    spine (which energizes the chakras), insert your thumbs
    one below the other in the indented spaces between the
    vertebrae. Extend your fingers outward and place them
    on the rib cage for support. Begin at the top of the spine.
    Breathe together and as you exhale gently push your
    thumbs inward, releasing pressure on the following inha-
    lation. Insert your thumbs in the next set of spaces and
    repeat down the entire length of the spine.

5. Hold your fingers firmly together and extend them out-
    ward. Insert your fingertips in the indented area on either
    side of the spine. Beginning at the upper spine, move
    your hand rapidly in a cutting or sawing motion. Work
    your way down the entire length of the spine, using this
    indented area as a pathway. Do the same thing on the
    opposite side.

6. Find the inner set of bladder meridians, which run along
    two parallel lines located about two finger-widths out

from the center of the spine. Using the thumb technique described in step four, press your thumbs along the length of the meridian, beginning at the shoulders and proceeding down the back and across the buttocks in one-inch steps. When massaging the rib cage, insert your thumbs in the spaces between the ribs.

7. Find the outer set of bladder meridians, which run along two parallel lines about two finger-widths out from the inner pair of meridians. Use the thumb technique described in step four to massage both sides simultaneously, from the shoulders to the buttocks.

8. Use the fingertips, thumb, and base of the palm to massage the receiver's shoulder blade. Continue with active massage for about one minute, loosening any tension in the surrounding muscles and tendons. Repeat with the other shoulder blade.

9. Place your thumb in the center of the shoulder blade. Breathe together with the receiver and press as you exhale, massaging this area with a quick circular motion. Repeat three times and proceed to the other shoulder blade.

10. Place both hands together across the spine in the region of the waist. Place your thumbs on one side and your fingers on the other side of the spine, as shown in Figure 3.5. Use a deep kneading motion to massage this area. Pain here is often a sign of expansion or tightness in the kidneys, and indicates potential weakening of sexual vitality.

11. Use your palm, fingers, and thumb to knead and rub the entire back, relieving any tension or stagnation in the muscles and along the meridians. Start at the upper region and massage down the periphery of the back, one side at a time. After you finish, smooth the flow of energy down the spine and both sides of the back.

12. To massage the buttocks, move slightly downward so that you can reach the indented area in the center of both sides of the buttocks. Push the base of your palms firmly

Figure 3.5   Massaging the Region of the Waist.

in this area and then massage in an upward and outward direction. Repeat for about one minute. This is especially good for strengthening sexual vitality. Then, place your hand on the tailbone. Use the base of your palm to gently pound the tailbone. Continue for about thirty seconds in order to send stimulation along the entire length of the spine.

PART THREE: THE ARMS AND HANDS

Six meridians run along the arm. Three—the lung, the heart governor (the comprehensive body function responsible for the circulation of blood and body fluids), and the heart—run down the inside of the arm from the armpit to the hand and out to the fingers. The other three—the large intestine, the triple heater (the body-wide function responsible for the generation of heat and caloric energy), and the small intestine—run from the fingers up the outside of the arm to the shoulder. See Figure 3.6 for a depiction of the meridians in the arm.

To energize the arms and hands, do the following.

1. Place your hand on the root of the arm with your thumb inserted in your partner's armpit and your fingers placed across the top of the shoulder joint. Grasp the wrist with your other hand and stretch the arm by pushing your hand down and gently pulling the arm outward with your other hand. Repeat several times.

2. Grasp the arm by placing both hands in the area between the wrist and the elbow. Using the shoulder as the axis of rotation, gently twist the entire arm first in one direction and then in the other. Repeat several times.

3. Place one hand above and the other below the elbow. Gently twist the upper and lower sections of the arm in opposite directions, as if you were wringing out a wet towel. Repeat by twisting each section in the reverse direction.

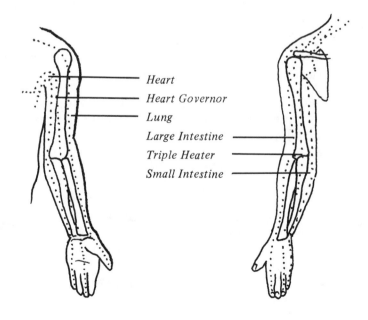

Heart
Heart Governor
Lung
Large Intestine
Triple Heater
Small Intestine

Figure 3.6   The Meridians in the Arm.

4.   Use the palm and fingers of your more active hand to press down both sides of the arm, making sure to loosen any tension in the muscles and tendons. Work your way down to the hands and fingertips.

5.   Imagine three parallel lines running about one-quarter of an inch apart along the inside of the arm from the armpit to the wrist. These correspond roughly to the heart, heart-governor, and lung meridians. Place one hand under the arm for support, and with the thumb of your other hand press along each line starting at the armpit and working your way down to the wrist. First massage the heart meridian, then the heart governor, and finally the lung meridian. As you massage down each line, spend extra time massaging the elbow and wrist portion with a gentle circular thumb motion.

6.   As with the above step, imagine three parallel lines running along the outside of the arm, this time in the opposite direction from the wrist to the shoulder. These lines correspond roughly with the large intestine, triple heater, and small intestine meridians. Using the same technique, massage down these outer lines from the wrist to the shoulder. Start with the large intestine and proceed to the triple heater and small intestine meridians.

7.   Support your partner's wrist with one hand, and with the other gently rotate the hand several times. Repeat in the opposite direction.

8.   Place the hand on one knee for support. Position the little finger of one of your hands between the thumb and index finger of their hand, and position your other little finger between their fourth and fifth fingers. Place your other fingers on the underside of the hand for support, and massage the palms by rapidly pressing your thumbs one after the other into the palm, working your way around the entire hand. Place special emphasis on the area adjacent to the thumb that corresponds to the digestive and respiratory systems.
       Pain or a reddish or bluish color in this area often

indicates swelling or fatty deposits in the intestines. Massage the center of both palms. This point, which is a part of the heart governor meridian, energizes the heart, stomach, and hara chakras as well as sexual vitality. Pain in this point frequently indicates that the heart and circulatory system is overworking and that a person may be experiencing sexual fatigue. Place one hand under their hand for support, and with the thumb of your more active hand, press the center of the palm and then release. Repeat several times.

9. Turn the hand so that the outside is exposed. Find the indented area between the thumb and index finger. Massage this area for about one minute, using a deep, circular thumb motion to release tension and stagnation. This area is along the large intestine meridian. Pain or tightness indicate stagnation or overexpansion in the large intestine.

10. Each of the fingers corresponds to one of the meridians that run along the arm in the following order: thumb— lungs; index finger—large intestine; middle finger—heart governor; ring finger—triple heater; little finger (inside)— heart; and little finger (outside)—small intestine.

    When massaging the fingers, imagine a series of five points, three located in the center of the three sections of each finger and two located immediately below the finger on the palm. (Use four points when massaging the thumb, two in the center of each section and two immediately below in the root of the thumb.) Grasp the wrist with one hand and turn the palm upward. Massage each finger separately by pressing each point with the tip of your thumb, rotating your thumb in a circular motion, releasing, and then proceeding to the next point. Start with the points located at the root of the fingers. Place your fingers on the opposite side of each finger for support. When you reach the last point on the tip of each finger, pull and rotate the finger several times.

11. Brush down both sides of the arm and out through the fingertips. Repeat several times.

Shift to the other side of your partner and massage the other arm using the above steps.

PART FOUR: THE LEGS AND FEET

The bladder, gall bladder, and stomach meridians run down along the back, sides, and front of the leg. The kidney, spleen, and liver meridians run up along the inside. It is of primary importance, when massaging the legs, to activate the flow of energy along these meridian pathways.

To massage the legs, do the following.

1. Have your partner lie on his/her stomach. Shift your position so that you are below the feet. In most cases, you will notice that the legs are not perfectly even. If one leg is longer than the other, this indicates a degree of imbalance between the right and left side of the body. It may also indicate that the pelvis is slanted in the direction of the longer leg, often the result of overexpansion in the organs located on that side, especially lower organs like the kidneys, intestines, and sexual organs.

    To help correct this imbalance, grasp the shorter leg below the ankle. Gently pull the leg slightly upward and outward, lower it to the ground, and then release.

2. Grasp both feet by holding the toes between your palms and fingers. Bend the leg at the knee, cross the feet at the ankles, and press them backward into the buttocks. If the legs and feet are painful or not flexible enough to do this, do not force them.

    With the legs in this position, reverse the feet and again press down into the buttocks. After you finish, return the feet to their normal position on the floor.

3. The bladder meridian, which runs down the back, continues down the back of both legs in the center and out to the fifth toe. Using the thumb, press down the meridian from the buttock to the ankle. Each leg may be massaged separately or both at the same time. Use a gentle penetrating pressure when massaging this meridian; however,

ease up when you reach the sensitive area behind the knee, as pressure here can be painful. If the receiver feels pain when you press the part of the meridian on the center of the calf that corresponds to the large intestine (as in Figure 3.7), his or her intestines are overexpanded, and energy in the hara chakra has become weak.

4. Raise one leg by bending it at the knee. Place one hand below the ankle and grasp the toes with the other. Begin to rotate the foot in a circular motion for about one minute in one direction and then in the other. Don't force the foot to rotate beyond the point at which discomfort is experienced. Pain or lack of flexibility in the ankles is a sign of hardening of the arteries and joints, and of a general decline in the conductivity of heaven and earth's forces.

5. With the leg in the above position, use one hand to press the foot downward so that it is parallel to the floor. (See Figure 3.8.) With the thumb and index finger of your

Figure 3.7   Pressing the Bladder Meridians.

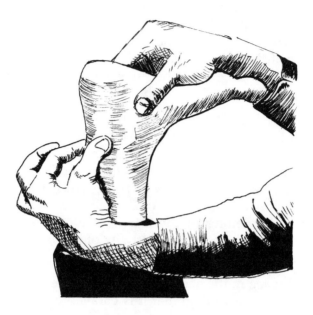

Figure 3.8   Massaging the Achilles Tendon.

other hand, massage the Achilles tendon by rubbing it
vigorously up and down. This tendon correlates to the
sexual organs. It should be tight and somewhat firm. If it
is loose, the sexual organs may have become weak as a
result of dietary excess. A coating of fat around the Achilles also suggests fat and mucus deposits in the sexual
organs. Massage the Achilles for about thirty seconds.
This helps energize sexual vitality.

6. Keeping the foot in the position indicated in step four,
    locate the region on the inside of the leg about four fin-
    ger-widths up from the ankle. Known in Japanese as the
    "junction of three yin meridians," this area corresponds
    to the spleen, liver, and kidneys. This region was used
    traditionally by Oriental doctors to treat disorders in the
    sexual organs but should not be massaged when a
    woman is pregnant. Use the thumb of your free hand to
    massage this region for about thirty seconds with a deep,
    but gentle, circular motion.

7. Actively massage the bottom of the foot by alternately pressing with the fingers of your left and right hands. Place your thumbs opposite to your fingers on the underside of the foot for support. Massage the entire sole of the foot for about thirty seconds in this manner.

8. Refer to Figure 3.9, which shows the kidney point on the underside of the foot. Known in Japanese as "bubbling spring," this point is where energy in the kidney meridian begins its course up the inside of the leg. Place your free hand on the opposite side of the foot for support and press the point with your thumb. You may also vibrate your thumb as you are applying pressure. Release pressure and repeat several times. If this point is overly sensitive or painful, the kidneys are not functioning at their optimum. A thick callous on the kidney point is caused by overintake of animal protein and fat and indicates that energy is not flowing smoothly along the kidney meridian and that sexual vitality is often below par.

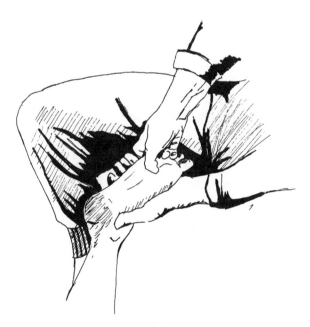

Figure 3.9   Applying Pressure to the Kidney Point.

9. Massage the toes by using the pinching technique described for the fingers. Work your way outward to the tip, and then pull and rotate each toe. When you finish each toe, pull excess energy out by gently pulling and snapping the tip.

    Each toe corresponds to a particular organ and meridian in the following order: large toe (outside)—spleen; large toe (inside)—liver; second and third toes—stomach; fourth toe—gall bladder; fifth toe—bladder. Each of these organs and their corresponding meridians are stimulated and activated when we massage the toes.

10. Supporting the foot from the underside, use your free hand to rapidly pound the entire bottom of the foot. Tighten your fingers into a fist and pound with the side of your hand. Like the head, palms, ears, and back, the bottoms of the feet correspond to the entire body, and the entire body benefits when we stimulate them.

After you finish the above steps, lower the foot to the floor and repeat steps four through ten with the other foot. After massaging both feet, brush your partner's energy down both legs from the buttocks to the toes.

PART FIVE: THE FRONT OF THE BODY

It is of primary importance, when massaging the front of the body, to stimulate the front organs directly along with the leg meridians. The meridians include those of the kidney, spleen, and liver, which run up the inside of the leg, and the stomach and gall bladder, which run down the front side. As this is a basic technique, just massage in the general vicinity of the meridians rather than trying to locate them precisely or to identify specific points.

To energize these meridians and organs, do the following.

1. Have your partner turn over so that he is lying comfortably on his back. Grasp both legs by the ankles and massage upward to the pelvis, generally loosening any tension in the muscles. Repeat this several times.

2. Imagine three parallel lines running up the inside of the leg from the ankle to the pelvis. These correspond roughly to the kidney, spleen, and liver meridians. Place your fingers on the outside of the leg for support, and press upward along each line with your thumbs. Each leg can be massaged separately or both can be massaged at the same time.

3. Imagine a line running down the top of the leg on the outside of the knee from the pelvis to the foot. This corresponds generally to the stomach meridian. Keep your hands in the position described above, only this time use your fingers to massage down the line, and use your thumb for support. The legs can be massaged one at a time or simultaneously.

4. Imagine a line running down the outside of the leg from the hip socket to the foot. This corresponds roughly to the gall bladder meridian. Using the above technique, massage down this line as well.

5. Have your partner raise his or her knees and place the feet flat on the floor. Place your hands on the knees and press the knees upward and then downward toward the abdomen, as shown in Figure 3.10. This helps release tension deep within the intestines. Return the legs to their resting position on the floor.

6. Place the fingers of your active hand together and extend them firmly outward. Place the tips of your extended fingers on the lower right side of the abdomen in the region of the ascending colon. Breathe together, and on the outbreath press gently into the abdomen. Release pressure with the following outbreath, and reposition your hand further up along the ascending colon. Repeat this procedure along the entire length of the colon, moving across the tranverse colon and then down the descending colon on the left side.

   Pain or hardness in the large intestine is often a sign of mucus, fat accumulations, or swelling due to the over intake of saturated fats, flour products, sugar, liquid, and

**Figure 3.10   Pressing the Knees to Release Tension in the
Intestines.**

overeating in general. This practice can be repeated several
times, as it is very good for promoting regularity in the
bowels and for releasing stagnation in the lower body,
thereby activating the flow of energy to the sexual organs.

7. Place your hands across the abdomen. Begin to gently
   knead and massage the small intestine. Continue for about
   a minute.

8. Place your thumbs under the rib cage. Breathe together,
   and on the outbreath gently press inward and upward.
   This step is very good for activating the liver, spleen, pancreas, and stomach. Repeat several times.

9. To complete the massage, place one hand lightly on your
   partner's abdomen and the other lightly on the forehead.
   Breathe together for a minute or two, or until he or she is
   completely relaxed. Detach your hands by raising them
   slowly upward.

CONCLUSION

If the massage has been done properly, your partner should feel relaxed yet energized. After you complete the massage, ask your partner to remain in a resting position for about five minutes. Meanwhile, wash your hands in cold water to remove any excess energy that you may have picked up during the massage. With this, your basic massage is now complete.

4.

Solving Sexual Problems

When the energies of heaven and earth flow smoothly through the body, love and sexuality bring joy and happiness into our lives. The important point in satisfying sex is deep, gentle, but strong stimulation of the body and mind. For this, good health and conductivity to the energies of heaven and earth are essential.

However, sometimes energy doesn't flow smoothly. If energy in the sexual organs and chakras is weak or blocked, a person may become unable to experience sexual fulfillment. When this happens, people often try a variety of things to compensate. They may try to activate energy by using other body parts in sex. If this does not generate enough energy, the couple may think it helpful to change positions. They intuitively use the poles of heaven and earth through various acrobatics to strengthen their charge, and they start to do yoga postures in bed. If they did them correctly, the charge might be satisfactory. But usually they do not, so they continue to try many different positions. In some cases they are successful in increasing the charge, but in many instances they are not.

The next thing the couple may try is intuitive massage. Using their fingers, palms, and so on, they rub and push each other's bodies in an attempt to stimulate energy flow. They instinctively feel that this might work to accelerate the flow of energy. But at this time they may not know which meridians or points to stimulate. If these techniques work, it may be because they accidentally stimulate the right places. But often they do not. Besides, even if they did know the right points to massage, in the heat of passion they would most likely forget.

Visualization, or creative imaging, is another technique employed when the flow of energy is stagnated. Either or both partners may use fantasizing to activate the midbrain, which in turn stimulates the other chakras, the nervous system, the endocrine glands, and ultimately the sexual organs. Sexual fantasizing is stimulated by the intake of coffee, spices, stimulants, tropical fruits, sugar, and other foods with strong upward energy. However, these foods weaken the flow of energy in the sexual organs and lower body, and diminish physical vitality. Their use may result in the inability to translate sexual imagination into reality or to respond to actual stimulation. In some cases, overconsumption of foods and beverages that are more yin than yang can cause a person to prefer fantasizing to actual sex.

If these attempts aren't satisfactory, some couples resort to even stronger methods of stimulation. They may turn to sado-masochism or so-called "kinky" sexual practices. Whipping, for example, represents an attempt to generate enough heat and energy to "fire" the chakras, and if conductivity becomes high, the charge may begin. In some cases, the couple may even try to reinforce the charge of energy with electronic devices.

These efforts are often unsatisfactory because they do not deal with the underlying cause of the problem. If we are healthy, our bodies should charge very easily, and simple, natural sexual acts create the necessary high charge of energy. But for many people today, this no longer happens. This is why people start to think, "There is something wrong with my wife or husband. Maybe if I found a new partner, sex would be better." So they have an affair with someone else and separation or divorce can easily follow. This kind of thinking is only harmful and ignores the source of the problem. Let's take a look at what factors besides diet affect sexual energy and how changes in lifestyle can revitalize our sex lives.

SEX AND THE MODERN LIFESTYLE

Although diet is the basic cause of sexual problems, other aspects of the modern lifestyle contribute. One is the relative lack of physical activity among people today. In many ways, modern living has become too soft and comfortable. Surveys show, for example, that the average family in the United States spends up to seven hours a day sitting in front of the television! Inactivity such as this causes energy flow to stagnate. Several generations ago people were much more active. They didn't need special exercise or workout programs. Since physical activity stimulates the flow of energy in the chakras, meridians, and throughout the body, regular exercise, including taking a half-hour walk every day, is recommended to energize sexual vitality.

The materials used in the home also have a subtle but real effect on the body's energy flow. Wood, for example, permits the forces of heaven and earth to stream more freely through the inside of the house, energizing and vitalizing the body, while metal and concrete block this natural flow. Not only do steel and concrete isolate us from the weather, they also cut us off from the flow of natural energy. Fluorescent lights, color TVs, and computer display terminals drain energy from the body. If we spend time under artificial light or in front of these machines, it is important to make balance by regularly spending time out of doors. Contact with nature activates energy flow and enhances sexual vitality.

The fabrics we wear also affect sexuality. Natural fabrics, especially cotton, allow the skin to breathe and exchange energy freely with the outside. Cotton is especially recommended for undergarments and for items that come into contact with the skin like bedsheets and pillowcases. Synthetics block the body's uptake and outflow of energy. They can make us feel tired and diminish sexual vitality.

How we eat can be just as important as what we eat in strengthening sexual vitality. Today, people are often too rushed to eat (and to enjoy sex) in a calm and relaxed manner. Chewing well helps slow us down, makes digestion more complete, and increases the absorption of food. Chewing helps

Foot Soaking

Overconsumption of meat, chicken, eggs, cheese, and other animal products frequently leads to the formation of callouses on the bottoms of the feet and toes. These formations represent the discharge of excessive protein and saturated fat, and interfere with the smooth flow of energy in the body. As we saw in the last chapter, each toe is part of a meridian that energizes a major organ. Moreover, certain points or locations on the bottom of the foot correspond to different parts of the body. The art of foot reflexology is based on these correspondences.

Soaking the feet helps soften these hardened deposits and allows energy to flow more smoothly through the meridians. Simply fill the bathtub with enough hot water to cover your feet. Place both feet in the tub and soak for about three minutes or until they become red or warm. This can be done every evening before bed to relax your body and to establish an active energy flow through the meridians and chakras. Walking barefoot on the beach, soil, or grass is also an excellent way to activate your sexual energy.

release stagnation in the digestive organs and chakras and increases our overall vitality and endurance. Complex carbohydrates such as those in whole grains, beans, and fresh vegetables are digested largely in the mouth through the interaction with saliva. For maximum health and vitality, chew each mouthful at least thirty to fifty times, and don't eat before bed, preferably for several hours. Food eaten before sleeping stagnates in the digestive system and lessens vitality and responsiveness.

Medical procedures can also weaken sexual vitality. When a woman conceives, for example, there is a great concentration of energy in the depths of the womb in the region corresponding to the hara chakra. If she then has an abortion, this energy suddenly disperses and the hara chakra and the organs it nourishes in the lower abdomen become weak and loose. This lessens her sexual vitality and reproductive ability.

The tonsils and adenoids correspond to the sexual organs. Their removal affects a person's sexuality. When someone has them removed, he or she may experience a decline in vitality, endurance, and patience, and a lessening of resistance to disease. People who have had such surgery often experience a general reduction of sexual vitality, especially when they eat an unbalanced diet. Whenever an organ, gland, or other part of the body is removed, the flow of energy throughout the body as a whole, including the energy that activates sexuality, is affected.

Modern methods of birth control also affect sexuality. Although they have recently become popular because of the fear of AIDS and other sexually transmitted diseases, condoms block direct contact between the penis and vagina and reduce the intensity of sensation and exchange of energy during sex. Condoms create an artificial barrier between partners and reduce the total release of energy experienced at the moment of orgasm. At the moment of ejaculation, for example, a condom prevents a woman from experiencing the sensations of warmth and pleasure provided by the ejaculated stream of sperm and seminal fluids. Healthwise, condoms are far safer than methods such as the birth control pill or IUD, and their use is advised for those who engage in casual relationships without knowing the background of their partners, because condoms help prevent the spread of HIV, the virus that causes AIDS. However, for monogamous couples, using condoms can be distracting.

Despite repeated warnings of serious side effects, the birth control pill, which was first made available in 1959, is still the most widely used form of contraception on the market. A variety of oral contraceptives are available and they differ in the type and dosage of hormone used. The most commonly used types can be divided into two major categories: the combination pill that contains both a synthetic estrogen and a synthetic progestogen, and the synthetic progestogen-only pill.

Excessive doses of estrogen, a more yin or expansive hormone, hinder the formation of egg cells, or ova, which mature
and develop by inward motion of follicles in the ovaries. A
variety of side effects, both short and long term, are produced
in the body when repeated doses, beyond the amount usually
produced by the ovaries, are taken. This happens because estrogen is carried throughout the body by the circulation of
blood and other body fluids.

These side effects include headaches due to expansion of the
brain cells; loss of mental clarity, caused by gradual expansion
of the inner midbrain region; irregular heart palpitation,
caused by a gradual expansion of the heart and blood vessels;
gradual weakening of the functions of the liver, kidneys,
spleen, and other organs; gradual irritation of the parasym-
pathic nerve function; and other symptoms, both noticeable
and subtle. Moreover, a number of recent studies have re-
newed concern over the link between birth control pills and
breast cancer. The side effects produced by synthetic estrogen
are generally more yin or expansive, and manifest differently
and in varying degrees from woman to woman because of
differences in constitution, diet, activity, and living conditions.

Progestogen is a more yang or contractive hormone, and
when the type of birth control pill that contains this hormone is
used, a woman's condition becomes progressively more constricted or tight. As a result, a variety of symptoms may develop. However, even if no symptoms seem apparent, oral
contraceptives have a gradually accumulating negative affect
on a woman's overall condition, including her sexual vitality
and responsiveness. For this reason, all women are advised to
avoid oral contraceptives if they wish to achieve optimal
health.

Intrauterine devices, or IUDs, are plastic or metal objects of
various shapes and sizes that are inserted through the cervix
into the uterus, where they remain. They interrupt the con-
stant flow of energy that is generated around the abdominal
energy center, or hara chakra, and which charges the fertilized
egg and keeps the embryo alive and growing. Because the IUD
disturbs the normal pattern of this electromagnetic flow, it

interferes with implantation of the fertilized egg and with embryonic growth.

IUDs also disturb the current of energy that flows through the entire body. When the flow of electromagnetic energy is disrupted, general fatigue and emotional irritability are often the result. Also, the natural response of the body is to try to eliminate unnatural obstacles from the uterus. This impulse causes physical and emotional tension and disharmony, which often spill over into a woman's relationships.

The rate of pelvic inflammatory disease (PID) has also been found to be much higher among women with IUDs. Pelvic disease is a common cause of infertility, and doctors have reported a sharp increase in female infertility during the time that IUDs were available. To maintain harmony between body and mind and the satisfying sex life that results from that harmony, IUDs are best avoided.

The diaphragm is safer than the pill or IUD. A diaphragm is used in combination with a sperm-killing agent such as a jelly or cream, which is applied to both sides of the device. However, these chemically synthesized jellies or creams cause undesirable side effects. These substances are extremely yin. They are absorbed through the wall of the vagina and cause the blood condition to become unbalanced. They are a common cause of irritation in the vagina that can make intercourse painful or unpleasant. Frequent use can create an allergic reaction and eventually nervousness, fatigue, and a diminished appetite for sex. To minimize these effects, it is advisable to douche with warm salt water after using a diaphragm with a spermicidal agent. As with condoms, diaphragms create an artificial barrier between the partners and interfere with the total exchange of energy during sex. Using them also disrupts the natural spontaneity of lovemaking.

Natural birth control, based on the cycle of ovulation, is by far the safest method. In this method, three days before ovulation, during ovulation, and three days after ovulation, intercourse is avoided. For natural birth control to work, however, a couple must know the exact time of ovulation. This is much easier when they eat well. Through the macrobiotic diet and way of life, a woman can establish a regular menstrual cycle that is in accordance with the twenty-eight-day cycle of the moon. Women who are more yang would menstruate at the full moon, while those who are more yin would menstruate at the new moon, although this pattern would vary.

Now that we have looked at how our lifestyles can affect our sexuality, let's see what the art of Oriental diagnosis can tell us about our sexual health.

ASSESSING SEXUALITY

In the book *Your Face Never Lies* (Avery Publishing Group, 1985), the ancient art of Oriental diagnosis was introduced. If we know what to look for, we can use Oriental diagnosis to reveal the condition of the body in the face, hands, feet, and other features that are readily apparent. The correspondences that exist between internal condition and external appearance make it easier to actually see how food and lifestyle affect sexuality, and can help us spot potential trouble areas before a condition becomes serious. In this section, we discuss some of the things that the face, hands, and other parts of the body tell us about sexual health.

Face

Below are some of the things that can be determined by observing facial characteristics.

- Strong, healthy-looking hair shows that a person's sexual vitality and reproductive ability are potentially sound. On the other hand, split ends show that sexual vitality has become weak due to overconsumption of yin extremes, including sugar, chocolate, alcohol, soft drinks, drugs, and medications.

- Hair loss that starts in the center of the head arises from overintake of yang extremes, including meat, eggs, cheese, poultry, and fish and seafood. It is often an indication that hard fat deposits are accumulating in the chakras, blocking the smooth flow of energy in the prostate gland and in the blood vessels that supply the penis.

- Eyebags that appear watery and swollen (loose and saggy) are an indication of an overexpanded condition in the kidneys, bladder, and sexual organs. This results from drinking too much liquid and eating too many extreme yin foods. Eyebags are usually a sign that sexual vitality has become weaker. This condition can be corrected by moderating liquid intake and avoiding yin extremes.

- Eyebags that appear fatty and swollen (dense and solid) indicate that mucus and fat are accumulating in the ovaries, Fallopian tubes, and uterus, and in and around the prostate gland. These conditions can be overcome by restricting the intake of mucus- and fat-forming foods, especially dairy products, meats, eggs, poultry, simple sugars, and oils.

- A small horizontal crease located between the eyebrows above the bridge of the nose indicates tightness in the pancreas. The flow of energy along the primary channel is often blocked as a result of this condition. The cause is overintake of poultry, cheese, eggs, shellfish, and other animal foods. Tightness in the pancreas often causes hypoglycemia, or chronic low blood sugar, and is accompanied by tension, fatigue, and anxiety.

- White or yellow mucus on the lower part of the white of the eye, below the eyeball, is an indication of mucus and fat accumulation in the lower part of the body, including in and around the hara chakra, intestines, ovaries, uterus, Fallopian tubes, and prostate gland. In women, it is often a sign of vaginal discharge, and in both sexes, of stagnation in the sexual organs.

- Hardening at the tip of the nose shows that saturated fat is accumulating in the prostate gland, weakening its contracting power, as well as in the blood vessels that supply the penis. This is caused by overconsumption of cheese, eggs, poultry, and other forms of animal food, and may indicate troubles with male potency. In women, it is an indication that mucus and fat are accumulating in the reproductive tract.

- A milky white color on the cheeks is caused by overintake of dairy foods or soy products, including soy milk. This condition shows a lessening of sexual vitality due to accumulation of mucus and fat in the reproductive organs. Pimples on the cheeks show that fat and mucus are being eliminated through the skin and that fat and mucus are accumulating in the corresponding internal region. In some cases, pimples are an indication of vaginal discharge or cysts in the reproductive tract.

- In women, a horizontal crease in the region between the mouth and nose indicates stagnation in the sexual organs resulting from overintake of animal foods. It may mean that a woman is suffering from PMS (premenstrual syndrome), irregular periods, or pain during menstruation.

- In men, the inability to grow a mustache is a sign that sexual potency is potentially weak. This results from overintake of milk, sugar, ice cream, tropical fruits, and other yin extremes, often from the time of childhood.

- In women, growth of a mustache is a sign of stagnation in the reproductive organs caused by accumulation of fat and mucus that can interfere with fertility and sexual vitality. The cause is overconsumption of cheese, milk, eggs, poultry, and other animal foods.

- Pimples around the mouth show that fat and mucus are accumulating in the reproductive organs, obstructing the flow of energy and weakening sexual vitality.

- A swollen lower lip indicates overexpansion in the intestines and hara chakra. It is a sign of stagnation in the intestines and lower body that results in diminished sexual vitality.

Hands and Feet

A person's sexual vitality may be determined by looking at certain signs present in the hands and feet.

- If you feel pain or tightness when you press the center of your palm, your sexual vitality is less than it could be. This condition indicates stagnation in the chakras and is caused by the overintake of simple sugars and fats and by overeating or overdrinking in general.

- Cold hands are also an indication that energy is not flowing smoothly through the primary channel and chakras, and this makes the spark of sexuality harder to generate. This condition is usually caused by overconsumption of sugar, fruit, concentrated sweeteners, and iced or cold foods or drinks, including ice cream and soft drinks. Raw fruits and vegetables, which cool the body, also have this effect. Cold hands are also an indication of sluggish or inactive circulation.

- Moist or wet hands indicate that the kidneys, bladder, and circulatory system are overworking due to the intake of an excessive amount of fluid. This is often a sign that a person's vitality, including their sexual vitality, is declining.

- Hard, dry skin on the hands (or the body in general) is caused primarily by the overintake of saturated fats. Accumulation of hard fat under the skin makes the meridians, chakras, and primary channel less conductive to the energy of heaven and earth. In men, it may indicate enlargement of the prostate, and in women, decreasing sensitivity in the sexual organs.

- A whitish color on the fingernails is often an indication of underactive circulation and low hemoglobin—anemia in general. Healthy nails are pink in color. This condition is caused by the overconsumption of refined flour, fruits, juices, sugar, and sweets. In some cases, overconsumption of salt, dried or baked foods, and animal products may cause a similiar condition, as can a lack of fluid. White nails are a sign that sexual and life vitality are declining.

- Splitting or chipping at the ends of the fingernails results from chaotic dietary habits and from the overconsumption of yin foods and drinks. It indicates weakness in the testicles and ovaries. A reddish color or swelling around the cuticle of the nail shows a similar weakening in the reproductive organs.

- Inflexibility in the ankle joint is a reflection of an overall lack of flexibility and vitality, including in matters relating to love and sex. This condition is caused by overintake of animal foods high in cholesterol and saturated fat.

- Swelling or fat around the Achilles tendon shows that fats and mucus are also accumulating in the reproductive organs. If the Achilles is flabby and loose, sexual vitality is weak.

- Cold feet are an indication that energy is not flowing smoothly through the chakras and body as a whole. The primary cause is overintake of extreme yin foods and beverages. It correlates with a decline of sexual vitality and poor circulation.

- Hard callouses on the bottoms of the heels show that the flow of energy in the sexual chakra and organs has become blocked or restricted due to overconsumption of animal fat and protein. It may be a sign of fat and mucus accumulation in the prostate gland or in the female reproductive tract.

Pelvic Hair

As with the head hair, the condition and quality of pelvic hair reveals the quality and nature of sexual energy and vitality.

- Thick pelvic hair shows generally sound sexual vitality and reproductive capacity.

- Thin pelvic hair is an indication of a more sexual sensitivity but less reproductive capacity.

- A wider area of pelvic hair shows the potential for less orderly sexual behavior, with a greater susceptibility to genital disorders.

- A smaller area of pelvic hair shows a generally sound condition and reproductive capacity.

- No pelvic hair is an indication of sexual sensitivity but less vitality and reproductive capacity.

Each person is a little different, but most of us are capable of full, healthy sexual relationships. Nearly every sexual problem can be improved with proper diet.

HEALTHY SEXUALITY

The way each person eats determines the quality of his or her sexual energy and abilities. Since food creates our biological energy and quality, it is important for couples to eat together, and to eat good-quality food. In this way, they establish a similar biological direction while keeping up their health. This makes it much easier to develop clear and open communication and shared intuition and common sense. From this foundation, a couple's lovemaking can develop from the physical to the mental and spiritual levels, enabling them to grow together for a lifetime.

There are two principles for eating that will help a couple achieve sexual happiness. The first is eating for compatibility. Unless a couple eats together often and shares a similar quality of food, they may become so unlike each other that communication and understanding become difficult, and separation could result.

The second principle for satisfying relationships is called "eating for attraction." Between men and women there should be some small differences in diet in order to strengthen the polarity that exists between them. This principle, however, should never override the first; unity is the origin of polarity and not vice versa.

To accentuate his conductivity to heaven's force, a man can occasionally eat more side dishes that have a slightly saltier taste, or that contain root vegetables, buckwheat, or low-fat white meat fish. He may also use a slightly larger volume of condiments, such as sea vegetable powder or gomashio, provided his condition does not become too tight. The male body is more hard and compact than the female body: it contains a higher portion of muscle and bone. Eating a slightly higher volume of animal food and more yang vegetable foods helps strengthen a man's masculine quality. At the same time, if he eats too many fruits, sweets, or foods with more yin energy, he risks weakening his masculine vitality.

Women, on the other hand, can eat a slightly larger volume of lightly cooked and seasoned dishes in order to accentuate the upward flow of earth's energy. A woman can take a little less salt and more lightly cooked vegetables, provided her condition does not become too weak or lacking in vitality. Less animal food is better, and foods such as tempeh (soy "meat"), tofu, and seitan (wheat "meat") can be included often as good sources of vegetable protein. The female body is softer than the male: it contains a slightly higher percentage of fat. She can therefore eat more of foods such as mochi (pounded sweet brown rice), amazake (rice milk), and others that contain good-quality fats and proteins. The naturally sweet taste provided by chestnuts, grain sweeteners, and cooked fruits can also be included more frequently than in a man's diet. Of course, it is important for women not to eat too many sweets or desserts—otherwise their vitality will start to diminish.

On the whole, the total volume of a man's intake may be a little larger than a woman's. Men also need a slightly larger variety of foods and tend to eat out more often. This is not necessarily harmful, provided they still eat at home most of the time, and when they do eat out, the quality of the foods they select is not too bad.

When couples first start going out together, and when they are first married, they tend to eat out more often; also, the husband may be more involved, at first, in helping with the selection of dishes cooked at home. Newlyweds or dating couples, therefore, are likely to eat more widely. But after a few years of marriage, and particularly after their first baby is born, a wife tends to gradually take the lead in planning meals for her family. At this stage in their marriage, couples often become concerned with finances and with keeping up their health, so they tend to eat at home much more and prefer simpler, well-balanced meals. As a result, they tend to grow closer and become more responsive to each other's needs.

Today, however, many couples don't experience genuine harmony in their relationships. Many experience problems in their sex lives, and this leads to trouble in other areas. Couples in this situation need to both reflect on and change their diets and ways of life. Even if the problem is due to the condition of one of the partners, we cannot isolate that partner and try to improve his or her condition without considering the couple as a unit. For optimal health, including a mutually satisfying sex life, both partners need to eat whole cereal grains as their principal food, totalling roughly half of their daily diet, together with side dishes prepared from the other categories of food presented in Chapter 2.

At the same time, foods or beverages that chill the body are best avoided, as are animal foods such as steak, hamburger, fried chicken, and grilled cheese sandwiches. When we eat foods such as these, fat gathers around the organs, chakras, and primary channel, making them hard, dulling our sensitivity, and blocking the flow of energy. Both partners need to center their diets on whole grains, with side dishes of beans, bean products, and sea and land vegetables that are properly energized through cooking. In this way, they create a stable, warm temperature and, as fats and other excessive factors are discharged from the body, energy will begin to flow smoothly and sexual vitality will return. The macrobiotic diet—based on eating in harmony with the environment and with human needs—lies at the heart of the recovery of sexual happiness.

If someone has undergone medical procedures such as the ones mentioned in the previous section, he or she can compensate to the maximum degree by eating a naturally balanced diet. Even if someone has damaged their nervous system and chakras with drugs or medications, health and vitality will eventually return, although recovery might take a little longer.

SPECIFIC SEXUAL PROBLEMS

So far we have been talking about diet and sexuality in general terms. Below, we turn our attention to the way that diet and daily life influence the development of specific problems, as well as their use in the recovery of sexual health.

Impotence

Impotence comes in a variety of forms. In one, sometimes referred to as primary impotence, a man is unable to achieve an erection that is firm enough to enter the vagina. In the other, sometimes called secondary impotence, a man cannot maintain an erection long enough during intercourse to ejaculate in the vagina or bring satisfaction to his partner.

About 20 to 30 million American men suffer from chronic impotence, a condition that becomes dramatically more prevalent as men get older. Among men in their twenties, for example, impotence is relatively rare; while nearly three-quarters of men in their late sixties are believed to have the problem.

In terms of energy flow, impotence results when blockage or stagnation exists somewhere in the body, especially in the region of the sexual organs, or when a man is unable to generate a sufficient charge of energy. In many cases, it is the result of both of these conditions. Energy blockages result primarily from the overintake of animal foods that contain saturated fat and cholesterol, while weak energy is often the result of too much sugar, chocolate, raw salad or fruit, spices, iced beverages, drugs and medications, and other extremes that deplete the body's reserves or energy. Impotence is largely the result of body-wide imbalance caused by improper diet.

Overconsumption of saturated fat and cholesterol frequently causes narrowing and obstruction of the blood vessels that supply the penis. This interferes with a man's ability to achieve and maintain an erection. During sexual arousal, nerves stimulate the *corpora cavernosa*, two rod-shaped bundles of spongy muscle that run along each side of the penis, to relax and draw in extra blood. As they expand, these chambers press shut veins that normally drain blood from the organ. Incoming blood is held in the chambers, and the penis becomes hard and erect. However, when the blood vessels that supply the penis are constricted due to the accumulation of fat and cholesterol, not enough blood will enter the penis to produce an erection. Men with high blood pressure, high cholesterol, and other cardiovascular conditions are more prone to develop this problem and also face greater risk of heart attack and stroke. This condition is often accompanied by hardening and enlargement of the prostate gland, which, as we saw in Chapter 1, also interferes with male potency.

Overconsumption of yin extremes can also lead to impotence. Extremes such as drugs, alcohol, tropical fruits, or refined sugar deaden and weaken the nerves that trigger relaxation of the corpora cavernosa. These items can also cause the veins that close and trap blood in the penis to become loose so that not enough blood is held in the chambers for erection to occur. Moreover, chronic overconsumption of yin extremes also contributes to enlargement of the prostate, diminishing its contracting power.

Impotence can be overcome by correcting these dietary imbalances, especially by avoiding foods that are high in saturated fat and cholesterol as well as the yin extremes such as sugar, tropical fruits, coffee, alcohol, and iced or chilled foods or beverages. The effects of dietary change are often rapid and dramatic. Men who are able to lower their blood pressure and cholesterol through diet can often restore potency within a relatively short period of time.

To restore potency, it is important to avoid extremes of both yin and yang in the diet. Meat, eggs, chicken, cheese, and other fatty animal foods are best eliminated, as are sugar, spices, alcohol, soft drinks, chocolate, ice cream, coffee, and other yin extremes. The dietary pattern presented in Chapter 2 forms the basis for the natural recovery from impotence, with only slight modification. Whole grains are preferred to flour products or cracked or partially milled grains. The latter, when eaten excessively, constrict and tighten the chakras and blood vessels and can cause mucus and fat to form throughout the body. Whole buckwheat (kasha) and buckwheat noodles (soba) increase sexual vitality and can be eaten once or twice a week along with other whole grain dishes.

It is also important that the majority of vegetables be cooked rather than eaten raw. Overconsumption of raw salad cools the body and weakens the charge of energy in the chakras and sexual organs. Moreover, tomatoes, potatoes, peppers, avocados, eggplant, and other vegetables that are members of the nightshade family or that have been cultivated in tropical climates can cause the blood vessels to become weak and overexpanded and are therefore best avoided. Vegetables with strong contracting energy, including carrots, burdock, daikon radish, turnips, and other roots, can be included daily, along with leafy greens and other varieties.

Low-fat white meat fish may be eaten on occasion, on average about once or twice per week, while the vitality stew described on page 93 can be eaten once per month (for three days in a row) for several months. Too much fruit (even temperate varieties, which are normally fine for occasional use) weakens the body's energy and sexual vitality and contributes to overexpansion of the blood vessels. Overconsumption of fruit, especially tropical varieties, can also dull and weaken nervous response. Cooking fruit with a pinch of salt helps make it more yang, and this is preferred until the condition improves. It is better to serve fruits only on occasion until potency is restored. Tropical and semitropical varieties are best avoided completely. Nuts, which are high in fats and oils, are best eaten in moderation only, or avoided until recovery is achieved. Tropical nuts, such as cashews and Brazil nuts, are especially high in fat and are best avoided. Lightly roasted seeds can be eaten on occasion as snacks.

Other than these slight modifications, the general dietary plan outlined in Chapter 2 can be followed to treat impotence. Of course, individual adjustments are always required and proper cooking is essential. Attending introductory programs such as the Macrobiotic Way of Life Seminar presented by the Kushi Foundation in Boston can be invaluable when making the transition to a macrobiotically balanced diet.

A naturally balanced diet is far less drastic than some of the more extreme approaches that men who experience impotence

Vitality Stew

In Oriental countries, a thick soup made with carp, burdock root, bancha tea leaves, miso, and ginger root has been traditionally used to restore vitality and sexual potency. The whole fish, including bones, scales, head, and fins, is cooked in the soup and becomes soft and digestible. The soup, known in Japanese as Koi koku (carp and burdock miso soup), is particularly warming in cold weather, but may be enjoyed all year even by those who ordinarily don't like fish or by those with a restricted intake of animal food. Vitality stew can be prepared as follows.

> *1 fresh carp (about 5 pounds)*
> *Burdock at least equal to the fish in weight*
> *1/2 to 1 cup used bancha tea twigs and leaves*
> *Bancha tea and spring water*
> *Miso to taste*
> *1 tablespoon grated fresh ginger*
> *Chopped scallions for garnish*

Select a live or freshly killed carp at a fish market. Ask the fishmonger to carefully remove the gallbladder and yellow bitter bone (thyroid) and leave the rest of the fish intact. This includes the scales, bones, head, and fins. At home, cut the entire fish into 1- to 2-inch-thick slices. Remove the eyes if you wish.

Then cut at least an equal amount of burdock root (ideally 2 to 3 times the weight of the fish) into thin slices or matchsticks. This quantity of burdock may take a while to prepare, so plan accordingly.

When everything is chopped, place the fish and burdock in a pressure cooker. Tie used bancha twig leaves and stems from your teapot in a cheesecloth—fresh leaves give the soup a bitter taste. The cheesecloth should form a pouch the size of a small ball. Place this ball in the pressure cooker on top or nestled inside the fish. The tea twigs will help soften the bones during cooking and make them more digestible. If the bones are not cooked long enough and remain hard, they may present a hazard when you try to swallow them. Therefore, make sure that the bones are cooked thoroughly and are completely softened.

Add enough liquid to cover the fish and burdock, approximately one-third bancha tea and two-thirds spring water. Pressure cook for 1 hour. Bring down the pressure, take the cover off, and add miso to taste (1/2 to 1 teaspoon per cup of soup) and grated fresh ginger. Simmer for 5 minutes. Garnish with chopped scallions and serve hot.

Variation: The burdock may be sautéed for a few minutes in dark sesame oil prior to cooking with the fish. Koi koku may also be made by boiling it in a heavy lidded pot for 4 to 6 hours, or until all the bones are soft and almost dissolved. As the liquid evaporates, more water or bancha tea should be added.

NOTE: If carp is unavailable, substitute another light fish, such as perch, red snapper, or brook trout. If burdock is scarce, use carrots instead, or use half burdock and half carrots combined.

Be careful to eat only a small amount at a time (1 cup or less). Otherwise, you will become overly attracted to liquids, sweets, and fruits. You can make enough for several days. Keep it in the refrigerator. You can take one bowlful per day for three days. This stew can be made once a month for several months until vitality is restored.

put themselves through today. For example, bypass surgery is sometimes recommended to bring in new sources of blood for men who have blood supply problems to the penis. Or, if not enough blood is being held in the penis and is leaking out, surgeons sometimes cut away small veins through which blood flows out of the penis. Sometimes drugs are injected that cause muscles in the blood vessel walls to relax and let blood flow into the penis just before intercourse, and penile implants and vacuum devices that are inserted in the penis are being used by some. However, all of these approaches deal only with the symptoms, not the problem. They don't deal with the underlying dietary and lifestyle causes of impotence. These approaches also disrupt the flow of energy in the body and can interfere with the natural spontaneity of sex.

The macrobiotic diet is ideal for achieving healthy blood pressure and low cholesterol. Studies conducted on several hundred people in the macrobiotic community in Boston by researchers at Harvard Medical School and the Framingham Heart Study have confirmed this scientifically. The mean blood pressure for the macrobiotic group was found to be significantly lower than that normally found in industrialized countries. Advancing age in this group had significantly less effect than in usual populations. Moreover, cholesterol levels for the macrobiotic group were also found to be much lower than usual U.S. levels, and these low levels were found in all age groups. The rise of cholesterol with age was very slight in the macrobiotic group, although it is usually significantly steep.

Consumption of animal food, including dairy products and eggs, was found to be the prime factor influencing cholesterol and blood pressure: the more animal food in the diet, the higher these levels were found to be. A more detailed description of these studies and of the macrobiotic approach to the prevention and recovery from cardiovascular disorders is presented in the book *Diet for a Strong Heart* (St. Martin's Press, 1985).

Not only does the macrobiotic diet prevent the development of high blood pressure and cholesterol, it can lower already high levels. Eating a naturally balanced diet can restore strength and elasticity to the blood vessels, help the prostate gland return to a normal, nonenlarged condition, and restore the sensitivity of the nerves that activate sexual response. Thousands of people around the world with high cholesterol and blood pressure have experienced a rapid return to normal within a short time after adopting a macrobiotic way of eating. They now enjoy excellent cardiovascular health—with little or no risk of heart disease—as well as optimal vitality and sexual potency.

Along with eating well, the way-of-life practices described earlier are also helpful in restoring potency. Daily body scrubbing energizes the body and breaks down deposits of fat in the blood vessels, under the skin, and in the prostate gland. It is also important to chew well and not to eat before sleeping, as this causes stagnation that interferes with the flow of energy to the sexual organs. Of course, exercise is helpful, as movement activates energy flow and helps speed the discharge of fats and other forms of excess from the body.

Impotence is not a male problem only. If a man has this problem, it is important for his wife or partner to encourage him to eat well and, ideally, to change her diet as well. Massage is also a good way for a spouse or partner to encourage the other and to open channels of communication and support. In this way, the energies of both partners blend more harmoniously, leading to better communication on all levels. Eating good-quality food together makes it easier for couples to talk openly about any problems or difficulties they may be having. Sharing healthful food creates a unity that fosters cooperation and the desire to solve life's problems together.

Premature Ejaculation

Differences between men and women are the result of the differences between heaven and earth. Heaven's downward force is stronger in men. It causes the male genitals to develop outside the body and the male physique to be more muscular and compact. It also stimulates production of the male hormone testosterone.

Earth's upward energy is stronger in women. It causes the female reproductive system to develop up inside the body and the female form to become softer and less angular than that of the male. It also stimulates the production of estrogen, the more expansive female hormone.

Heaven and earth are also responsible for the differences

Ginger Compress

Among the many home care practices used in macrobiotics, the ginger compress can be helpful in restoring sexual vitality and potency. The compress can be applied several times per week for a month or so or until sexual vitality is reestablished. To prepare the ginger compress, you will need a medium-sized piece of fresh ginger root (available at most natural food or Oriental markets), a flat metal grater, some cheesecloth, three medium-sized cotton towels, and a medium-to-large pot with a lid.

Grate the ginger root and place a clump about the size of a golf ball in a double layer of cheesecloth. Tie the cheesecloth at the top to form a sack. Then put a gallon of water in a pot and bring it up to, but not over, the boiling point. Just before the water starts to boil, turn the flame down to low.

Hold the cheesecloth sack over the pot and squeeze as much of the ginger juice as you can into the water, then drop the sack into the pot. Make sure the water doesn't boil, because boiling weakens the effect of the compress. Place the lid on the pot and let the ginger sack simmer in the water for about five minutes.

Fold one of the towels lengthwise several times so that it becomes long and thin. Hold it at both ends and dip the middle portion into the hot ginger water. Wring the towel out tightly, and if it is too hot to place on your skin, shake it slightly. Then place the hot towel on the area you wish to treat and cover it with one of the dry towels to reduce heat loss. With the hot towel still in place, prepare another ginger towel in the same manner. Apply it as soon as the first towel cools and repeat the procedure, alternating hot towels, every two or three minutes until the skin becomes red and/or warm.

Ginger compresses work by stimulating circulation, dissolving stagnation, and activating specific areas of the body. To help activate sexual potency, the ginger compress can be applied to the base of the spine in the area of the tailbone, or to the middle back in the area of the kidneys. Since this area is difficult for someone to reach by themselves, it is better if the person receiving the compress lies comfortably on his stomach, while his partner applies the compress.

After the ginger compress is complete, it is also helpful to scrub the entire body with a hot ginger towel. Simply dip one of the towels used for the compress into the pot of hot water, wring it out, and use it to scrub the body. When the towel cools, reheat it by simply dipping it into the pot of hot water. Also, soaking the feet in the pot of hot ginger water is a wonderful way to energize the flow of energy through the meridians, chakras, and body as a whole. Simply soak the feet in the hot ginger water for three to four minutes.

The ginger compress is fine for use by normally healthy adults as a part of home health care. However, it should not be applied in cases of fever or inflammation. Also, it is recommended that persons suffering from cancer or other serious illnesses use a milder application, such as a warm hot water compress, unless advised to do otherwise by a qualified macrobiotic teacher.

One pot of hot ginger water can be used for two days of compresses and body scrubs. Simply reheat the water before using it (don't bring it to a boil).

that exist in the way that men and women respond sexually. On planet earth, the ratio between heaven's and earth's forces is not equal. Heaven's downward force is generally seven times stronger than earth's expanding energy. That is why things fall downward, and why in human beings the head (which is created by earth's force) is generally one-seventh as long as the rest of the body (which is created by heaven's force). Cereal grains also reflect the one to seven ratio in the proportion of nutrients they contain.

Male sexuality is governed by this powerful charge of heaven's energy. That is what creates the male sexual drive. However, for many men, learning to control the rapid buildup of energy is the key point in becoming a mature and effective lover. A woman's sexuality is animated by earth's force. Her sensory focus covers a wider area than a man's, and she takes longer to build to orgasm. For sex to be mutually satisfying, both partners need to understand these differences and orient their lovemaking accordingly. A man especially needs to be sensitive to the needs of his partner and to allow enough time for her excitement to reach the level of his own.

Learning how to activate chakras other than the sexual chakra makes ejaculatory control much easier. The midbrain, for example, controls the flow of heaven's force along the primary channel, and governs the quality of energy received by the lower chakras. This means that a man can use his consciousness, which is centered in the midbrain, to control the buildup and release of energy in the sexual chakra and organs. If, for example, a man regulates the speed of his breathing, and centers it deep within the abdomen—in the area corresponding to the hara chakra—ejaculatory control becomes easier and more natural. Another way to control the buildup of energy in the sexual organs is to regulate the speed and intensity of movement during intercourse. Movement increases the charge of energy in the penis, so in order to delay the onset of orgasm, a man can continue gentle movement until he feels close to orgasm and then temporarily stop or slow down. If he continues with the pattern of tension and relaxation, it is easier to delay orgasm until his partner experiences it as well.

The buildup of erotic tension and excitement occurs in the form of an inward spiral in which energy from the periphery of the body gathers toward the centrally located chakras and sexual organs. At the beginning of a romantic encounter, the exchange of energy occurs mostly through the more yin, vibrational senses of sight and hearing. As the spiral winds inward, the focus shifts to the more yang, physical sense of touch. At

Stimulating the Chakras

Both partners can do a variety of things to activate the chakras when they make love. A few suggestions are presented below, but please experiment and discover your own techniques.

The uppermost chakras, especially the midbrain, process all incoming impulses, and are thus stimulated by every action taken during sex. However, things such as mouth-to-mouth kissing, kissing the cheeks, ears, or face, gentle cheek-to-cheek or nose-to-nose touching, and gentle stroking of the face, head, ears, and hair are especially stimulating.

The throat chakra is especially stimulated by gently caressing or kissing the neck or shoulders, as well as by mouth-to-mouth kissing and the other techniques presented above. Also, the sighs and other sounds of pleasure generated here add to the excitement and intensity experienced by both partners.

The feelings of love, warmth, and acceptance that originate in the heart chakra are especially brought forth by gently embracing, kissing, and caressing the upper body, including the neck, chest, and upper back; by gentle stimulation of the breasts and nipples through caressing or kissing; and by gently caressing or kissing the arms, hands, fingers, and particularly the center of the palms. Words of love, spoken with tenderness from the heart, also stimulate and activate this chakra.

The stomach chakra can be stimulated by gently caressing, kissing, or stroking the abdomen, middle back, and legs, especially the inner part of the thighs. The liver, spleen, and kidney meridians run up along the inside of the thighs and feed into and nourish the stomach chakra. Gentle caressing with the fingertips in an upward direction *toward the genitals is especially stimulating and exciting and also activates the hara and sexual chakras.*

The hara and sexual chakras are especially stimulated by gently caressing the lower abdomen and pubic region, lower back, buttocks, or legs. These chakras are also stimulated by gently touching and caressing the sexual organs.

first, couples touch casually—beginning at the periphery of the body—and progress to intimate touch.

As lovemaking continues, the initial stages of the spiral feed into and nourish those that follow, so that energy generated at the periphery of the body and in the upper chakras gathers toward the center of the body and lower chakras. The spiral reaches its climax at the moment of orgasm. (The word orgasm comes from the Greek word meaning "to boil" and implies the dramatic and sudden release of energy.) At that moment, the movement of energy reverses itself. Energy is suddenly released and discharged back out along the pathways it took to come in. A centrifugal spiral is created, and in this spiral energy moves in the opposite direction. On the whole, the body changes from a state of increasing heat and tension to one of increasing coolness and relaxation.

The convergence of energy during intercourse frequently occurs in the following stages.

1. Visual exchange and stimulation, as well as the direct non-physical exchange of energy between the meridians and chakras of both partners.

2. Stimulation and exchange through words, voice, and expression.

3. Casual touch, including hand to hand, hand to shoulder, arm to waist, etc.

4. Intimate touch, including kissing, head-to-head contact, hand-to-body contact, and mouth-to-body contact.

5.   Gentle touching and exploration of the genitals.

6.   Genital-to-genital contact.

7.   Orgasm.

From an energy standpoint, foreplay is a way of charging and activating the body's energy pathways, including the skin and meridians, and through them, the primary channel and chakras. Gentle foreplay also releases blockage and stagnation in these channels and causes sexual tension and excitement to build. It involves a wide area of the body in the sexual experience, and makes orgasm intensely enjoyable.

When a man ejaculates too quickly, however, these stages are often condensed or skipped. This condition, known as premature ejaculation, is defined clinically in a number of ways. Masters and Johnson define it as being unable to delay ejaculation long enough so that the female partner has an orgasm 50 percent of the time. Other sex therapists define it as not being able to hold off ejaculation for thirty seconds to a minute after starting intercourse. Although no one has actual figures, premature ejaculation is thought to be the most common male sexual problem, affecting millions of men and their partners.

Premature ejaculation occurs in a pattern that is the opposite of impotence. It tends to be more of a problem among younger men and less so among older ones, while impotence is rare in young men and increases with age. To some extent, this is natural: men tend to gain ejaculatory control as they mature, while young men are generally more impulsive when it comes to sex.

Dietary imbalances play an important role in premature ejaculation, as they do with impotence. The foods we eat affect our physical condition, and just as importantly, our attitudes about sex. Overconsumption of animal protein and fat makes ejaculatory control more difficult to achieve. When eaten excessively, these foods accelerate production of testosterone. This more yang hormone creates sexual tension and the desire for release. In extreme cases, overproduction of testosterone, resulting from an unbalanced diet, can trigger outbursts of violent, abusive, or uncontrollable behavior. Rapists and sex offenders, for example, have been found to have high levels of testosterone in their blood. These men are often given synthetic estrogens to neutralize their aggressive tendencies. However, this unnatural approach causes a variety of negative side effects and does not correct the underlying cause of the problem. A better approach is to rebalance hormone levels through dietary change in the direction of macrobiotics.

Eating too much protein also accelerates sperm production, further adding to sexual tension. Some men with this condition turn to physical activity to discharge built-up energies. Others turn to masturbation for release. Both a high rate of sperm production and elevated testosterone levels create the tendency to rush through sex with few preliminaries and less involvement of the upper chakras, including the emotions.

Of course, the effects of overconsuming yang extremes are often neutralized by the intake of yin extremes. The buildup of sexual tension caused by the overintake of meat, eggs, cheese, and other animal foods is often dissipated by sugar, spices, chocolate, ice cream, and drugs. So even though animal foods may create the desire for sex, the intake of yin extremes robs many men of the ability to have this desire. The temporary impotence caused by drinking too much alcohol is but one example of these more yin effects.

Another effect of the overconsumption of animal foods is to decrease the sensitivity of the skin, thus reducing one's sensitivity to the environment, including the needs of one's partner. In their research, Masters and Johnson encountered men with the problem of premature ejaculation who seemed incapable of thinking of their partner's needs. They considered themselves adequate lovers and believed the fault was their partner's. Some held to the notion that sexual pleasure was for the male only and was something that a woman should not expect.

Although social attitudes reinforce incorrect notions such as these, the underlying cause is insensitivity resulting from an unbalanced way of eating, especially overconsumption of animal foods. The overintake of milk, butter, yogurt, cheese, and other dairy products contributes to this insensitivity and to immaturity in relationships with others, including one's sex partners. Human milk is a suitable food for babies and at this stage of development it is normal for someone to be ego-centered in relation to others and concerned mainly with their own wants and needs. However, growing up means awareness of and consideration for the needs of people other than ourselves, and this normally develops as we stop drinking mother's milk and begin to eat grains and other foods of vegetable origin.

How we are nourished as infants affects not only our physical development but our temperament and character as well. The proper way to nourish human infants is naturally, at the mother's breast. Not only is breast milk nutritionally superior to cow's milk, but breastfeeding creates strong physical and emotional bonds between mother and baby. If infants are denied this opportunity and are instead fed by bottle, they may have difficulty establishing sensory-emotional bonds later in life. They may come to view sexual relations as simply a means of immediate pleasure and a release of pent-up energy.

Hypoglycemia, or low blood sugar, also contributes to premature ejaculation. As we saw in Chapter 2, overconsumption of animal foods causes tightness and the buildup of hard fats in the pancreas, making it harder for the organ to secrete anti-insulin, the hormone that naturally raises blood sugar. If blood sugar levels are normal, the body functions smoothly and the mind, emotions, and consciousness act as an integrated whole. However, when a man is suffering from hypoglycemia, he experiences an internal stress situation.

Low blood sugar levels have an acute effect on the functioning of the brain (which is the largest consumer of glucose in the body) and thus on our ability to function sexually. Low blood sugar elicits a shutting down of brain functions that are biologically less essential to conserve the more essential, mechanical functions necessary for survival. The less essential is the cerebellum, which controls the more refined, higher levels of human behavior including love, compassion, humor, and reasoning ability. When this is shut down, a person tends to revert to irrational behavioral tendencies governed by the cerebrum, which regulates breathing, heart action, and muscular activity in the "fight or flight" category, also known as the panic response. If an acute shortage of blood glucose occurs during sex (making love requires a great deal of energy), the result could be impotence or loss of the desire or ability to control ejaculation. As the higher brain centers shut down, sex becomes less of a conscious activity and more of an autonomic reflex governed by the senses.

Yin extremes such as sugar, chocolate, tropical fruits, spices, and others can also produce rapid ejaculation. These foods activate the more yin peripheral nerves, including those in the penis, making them hypersensitive to touch and other forms of stimulation. They also weaken the more yang central nervous system (which includes the brain and spinal cord and which is the seat of consciousness), and the ability to control the release of sexual energy. It is much more difficult for a man in this hyperstimulated state to delay the onset of orgasm, and the result is often premature ejaculation.

The solution to premature ejaculation is simple. The first step is to restore a balanced condition and energy flow through natural diet and way of life. When a man has a history of this problem, even if he tries his best, it is very difficult to control ejaculation when his blood chemistry, hormones, and body energy are working against him. Meat, eggs, dairy products, and other animal foods that contain plenty of saturated fat and cholesterol are best avoided, as are simple sugars such as refined sugar, honey, maple syrup, tropical fruits, and others that cause a quick but short-lived burst of energy. In their place, complex carbohydrates can comprise the mainstay of the diet. These provide the slow, steady release of energy necessary for endurance and staying power.

The macrobiotic dietary pattern presented in Chapter 2 is ideal for establishing the underlying condition that makes ejaculatory control easier to achieve. Among the whole grains recommended as principal foods, it is a good idea to mimimize the intake of baked flour products, as these promote tightness and stagnation throughout the body, including in the pancreas, thus contributing to hypoglycemia. Cracked or milled grains, including rolled or cut oats, are also best kept to a minimum, as they can cause mucus to form in the body, thus dulling sensitivity and blocking the flow of energy. Whole millet, which helps stabilize blood sugar levels, and whole barley, which helps dissolve internal hardening produced by animal fats, can be used several times per week in addition to brown rice and other grains.

Sweet vegetables, as we saw earlier, contain plenty of complex carbohydrates that accelerate recovery from hypoglycemia. They can be included daily along with a wide variety of other cooked vegetable dishes. The sweet vegetable broth described earlier can also be taken daily or often until the condition improves.

Beans, bean products such as tofu and tempeh, sea vegetables, and soup can be eaten daily as suggested in Chapter 2. Also, low-fat white meat fish can be eaten several times per week, as can cooked locally grown fruits. As we have seen, too many raw fruits and vegetables chill the body and weaken sexual vitality and energy, and it is recommended that their intake be minimized until ejaculatory control is restored.

When dealing with a problem such as premature ejaculation, it is important that both partners feel free to discuss their sexual needs with each other. Often, when couples experience sexual problems, they are hesitant or afraid to approach each other about it, and this underscores the difficulty that many couples have in communicating with each other in general. It may also be a good idea for the couple to change their approach to making love. Methods of foreplay and chakra stimulation, described earlier, can help broaden both partners' sensory focus and involve more of the body, mind, and emotions in the experience. It is important for men who experience premature ejaculation to practice giving and receiving gentle body-wide stimulation during sex, as this helps reduce the one-sided preoccupation with male orgasm.

When discussing sexual problems, there is a way to do it so as not to make one's partner feel hurt or insecure. Begin by reaffirming your love and appreciation for your partner and then gradually get around to the issue you wish to discuss. Also, don't end the conversation there, but go back to other issues before you finish. Make it clear that you are committed to helping your partner solve the problem, and that you love him in spite of it.

If the man is aware of the problem and wants to solve it, of course the situation is much easier. He will most likely be more open to exploring dietary change and other lifestyle modifications as a way of solving it. When a man is unaware that there is a problem, or is not open to talking about it, the situation is more complicated. In this case, the wife or partner may have to initiate helpful changes in diet over a longer period of time and slowly bring the subject up for discussion. She can also state that the dietary changes she is proposing are for reasons of overall health, including reducing the risk of degenerative illnesses such as heart disease and cancer.

The basic massage routine presented in the previous chapter can be a wonderful way to establish communication and to release excess energy. It can be used to help the man relax, melt away tension, and feel active and refreshed. The love meditation presented in Chapter 1 is also excellent in helping both partners become more attuned to each others' physical and emotional needs. Daily body scrubbing, regular exercise, and the other lifestyle suggestions presented earlier can also help tremendously in releasing stored energy, increasing sensitivity, and restoring overall vitality.

Difficulty in Achieving Orgasm

The differences between men and women are reflected in the problems that each have with sex. For many men, delaying orgasm is the primary issue, while for many women, having orgasm is most important. This is another example of the complementary relationship that exists between the sexes.

When a woman is consistently unable to have an orgasm, even when adequate stimulation is provided, the problem can be understood in terms of the flow of energy throughout her body. Some women have not experienced orgasm by any method, including intercourse, while others are able to have an orgasm through methods of stimulation other than intercourse. Some are able to have orgasms only on occasion and after many unsuccessful attempts. Energy blockages due to unbalanced dietary or environmental influences are the major cause of these problems. As we saw in Chapter 1, female sexuality is activated primarily by the upward, expansive force of the earth. Certain foods carry a strong opposite charge, especially meat, eggs, cheese, poultry, and other animal foods. Eating them produces hardening or tension in the body that blocks the natural unfolding of female sexuality.

Environmental influences also affect the flow of energy in the body. The attitudes toward sex, love, and affection that a woman is exposed to in childhood are particularly influential. For example, during childhood some women are taught that sex is somehow wrong, dirty, or sinful, while others are told that sex is an unpleasant chore that a wife has a duty to perform for her husband, without expecting pleasure or satisfaction of her own.

Psychological and Emotional Energy Blocks

These and other misconceptions about sex create psychological and emotional blocks that constrict the chakras and inhibit the smooth flow of heaven and earth's forces through them. Actually, love and sex are no more wrong or sinful than the natural bonding that occurs between hydrogen and oxygen which results in the creation of water molecules. When both partners are healthy and love each other, sexuality can serve as a means to realizing oneness with the universe and to elevating consciousness and spirituality.

If a woman is reared in an environment that is lacking in love, warmth, and affection, it is often difficult for her to express these emotions later in life, and this inhibits the natural unfolding of her sexuality. Also, if parents are often critical of their children, frequently belittling or humiliating them, the children may grow up lacking confidence in themselves, and this also interferes with their relationships and sexual abilities. And, if parents frequently argue and fight with each other (especially in front of the children), and eventually separate or divorce, when the children become adults they may have trouble trusting another person enough to allow their sexuality to come forth in a natural and uninhibited way.

Sexual problems happen when these negative psychological influences combine with the physical imbalances that result from an extreme diet. The degree to which these influences interfere with healthy sexuality, or the extent to which they can be overcome, depends largely on the person's underlying physical condition and adaptability. No two people have exactly the same attitudes and abilities in regard to sex, even if they were raised in the same household. Individual differences are due to the differences in physical constitution and condition that exist between people, and these result largely from each person's unique dietary habits.

A variety of other negative emotions interfere with love and sexuality and the ability to have an orgasm. Fear is a negative emotion that cancels sexual excitement and the yearning to become one with another person. Fear of pregnancy; fear of herpes, AIDS, or some other sexually transmitted disease; fear of rejection; fear of not having an orgasm or of having it too quickly; and fear of not being sexually attractive are just a few of the fears that men and women experience today. Suspicion, or lack of trust in one's partner, also counteracts the impulse toward love and sexuality and causes many people to abandon the pursuit of sexual happiness. Anger, hostility, or resentment also inhibit the ability to be compassionate and loving and to enjoy sexuality in its fullest dimensions.

Negative emotions arise from two sources: external or environmental influences, including the attitudes toward love and sex that are prevalent in society; and internal biological responses that arise largely as the result of what people eat. Much of the fear, suspicion, and resentment that people experience today can be traced to the unnatural separation between love and sex that characterizes modern society. Love and sex, once considered inseparable, are now regarded as separate functions—sex dealing more with the body and senses, and love with the mind and emotions. By separating sex from procreation, modern birth control has contributed to this tendency. As a result, sex has become much more "casual" than it used to be. However, sex without love eventually leads to feelings of emptiness and incompleteness.

It is difficult for women to experience happiness and fulfillment in their relationships if they do not love their partner. Men are more influenced by biological and sensory drives, and are capable of ignoring their feelings and acting as if love and sex were separate. This is especially true when a man's emotional and spiritual capacities are being limited by his way of eating. When a woman consents to casual sex, however, especially when her partner is selfish and inconsiderate as is often the case when love is not involved, she can easily begin to feel that she is being used. Naturally, emotions such as anger, hostility, and resentment can arise from these experiences.

Society frequently places too much emphasis on sex and not enough on love. Part of this can be traced to the false notion that unless you sleep with someone, you can't know them well enough to have a serious relationship with them. As a result, sex has become a precondition for marriage and the standard by which men and women evaluate one another. This creates a tremendous amount of anxiety to be sexually attractive and competent, and can lead to "comparison shopping" in what has become the modern equivalent of the sexual supermarket. Also, at the beginning of a relationship, men will often pressure their girlfriends to sleep with them as a way of "proving" their love. Many women consent more out of fear of losing their partner than out of a genuine desire to begin a sexual relationship.

The casual availability of sex in the modern world, including the ease with which relationships begin and the ease with which they are dissolved, creates an atmosphere that contributes to the insecurity that pervades many relationships today.

Moreover, within the realm of sex itself, emphasis is often placed on the physical aspects, especially orgasm, so that other dimensions of sexuality are overlooked. This often leads to an unnatural preoccupation with orgasm and to thinking of it as purely a mechanical reaction to erotic stimulation. In extreme cases, achieving orgasm can become an obsession that prevents a woman from letting go and losing herself in the sexual experience. By trying too hard to achieve orgasm, she may actually be lessening her chances of experiencing it. She may also feel anger and resentment if orgasm doesn't occur as she expected.

Another common cause of the inability to have an orgasm happens when a woman is not able to fully love or identify with her partner. In *Human Sexual Inadequacy,* Masters and Johnson cite this as the most common cause of what they termed "orgasmic dysfunction." It occurs among married couples or those involved in long-term relationships. Underlying many of these situations is a condition of biological (and energetic) incompatibility that is largely the result of differences in diet. If a woman's energy and physical qualities don't match those of her partner, it is often more difficult for her to respond sexually.

The Importance of Sharing Diet, Values, and Love

Everyone has a different physical and energetic quality. Some people are physically active and muscular, while others are artistic or intellectual. If a very active, muscular person marries a more sensitive artistic type, it could be difficult for their energies to harmonize and merge with each other. When it comes to sex, the muscular person would probably prefer a quick and direct approach, while their sensitive partner would probably like a slower, more gentle approach. Their energies are mismatched.

Generally, we can divide people into two broad categories depending upon the type of constitution and condition they have: those whose makeup is formed largely by eating plenty of meat and animal food; and those whose makeup is formed primarily by vegetable quality food, including grains and vegetables. Of course, an endless variety of types exist within these broad divisions. For example, within the animal food group there are steak and alcohol types, hamburger and diet soda types, cheese and wine types, fried chicken and ice cream types, and so on. Among the vegetable-eating group there are raw fruit and vegetable types, cooked grain and vegetable types, vegetable food plus some fish and sushi types, salad plus cheese and egg types, and so forth.

The exchange of vibrations between two people begins as soon as they touch hands or fingers. A man will receive vibrations from the woman and she will receive vibrations from the man. Actually, subtle vibrational exchange begins before this, and takes place when two people talk with each other in the same room. We usually experience this exchange in the form of the feelings or impressions that someone gives us. If their energies and biological qualities match, then there is no problem. But if they are very unlike each other, communication is difficult and one or both may begin to feel drained or frustrated even after talking for only a few minutes.

If contact becomes intimate, including sex, it can leave both parties feeling exhausted, heavy, or depressed. Actually, this outcome is the opposite of that which follows healthy sex. Sex is the charging and fusion of opposite energies, and should make both parties feel refreshed and happy. If this feeling is missing, the quality of the experience has not been good.

If someone is eating meat and sugar and has high cholesterol and blood pressure, and his or her partner is eating grains and vegetables and maintaining clean, healthy blood and a cholesterol below 150 milligrams, then the condition of their skin will be different. The first person will have rough skin, and the second will have more delicate skin. Their attitudes toward sex and manners of approaching it will also be different. Naturally, a mismatch of this type can cause a woman to tighten up in bed, blocking the flow of heaven and earth's forces through her body and making the experience of sex less enjoyable.

A related problem arises when two people don't share the same values and view of life, or when there is a wide gap in their level of thinking. For example, if a woman is more intellectually oriented and her partner is more sensorial, so that they don't share stimulating thoughts and ideas, she may find it hard to identify with him enough to fully enjoy sex. Or, if she is interested in pursuing the development of her consciousness and spirituality and he is concerned only with making money and is not open to her ideas, she may also have trouble experiencing sexual fulfillment. Again, the energies of both partners don't match.

These problems underscore a basic flaw in our modern sexual value system. For many in the modern world, the priorities in regard to love and sex are upside down. Sexuality is a delicate flower nurtured by love, caring, and commitment to another person. It is an important aspect of a relationship to be sure, but not the only aspect of a relationship. Trying to isolate sex from love is like trying to charge the lower chakras while stopping the flow of energy in the upper ones. If we deny the emotional and spiritual dimensions of our sexuality, we cut ourselves off from our true natures. Sexual unhappiness is the natural outcome of our spiritual blindness.

The Effects of the Modern-Day Diet

To a large extent, these values, which contribute to the difficulty to achieve orgasm, are the product of the modern diet and way of life. A diet centered on animal foods causes people to take in plenty of hard, saturated fat. A high-fat diet promotes such things as hardening or drying of the skin, accumulation of fat in and around the chakras and organs, and the stagnation of energy flow throughout the body. These conditions dull our sensitivity to more refined or subtle forms of vibration and make us more dependent upon the senses. We also crave stronger and stronger forms of stimulation to compensate for our dulled sensitivity. A denial of love and an overemphasis on sensory stimulation are often the results of this condition.

Also, because fat deposits block the skin, meridians, and other channels through which feelings and emotions (which are forms of energy) are naturally discharged, stored or pent-up energies often come out explosively in the form of anger or abusive behavior. This creates an undercurrent of violence that poisons the atmosphere and undermines trust between people, including between sexual partners. Fear of violence or abuse prevents many people from entering into relationships. It also causes many to stay in relationships that aren't working.

On an individual level, negative emotions are reinforced by dietary imbalances. Overconsumption of meat, eggs, cheese, poultry, and other animal foods makes the body tense and tight and creates internal stress. In this stressful condition, it is harder for someone to let go of negative feelings such as anger, fear, or resentment. As we have seen, energy blockages interfere with the discharge of negative emotions and dietary extremes also fuel negative feelings. As a result, negative emotions are internalized and held on to, and build into more or less permanent feelings.

Underlying this process for most people is a condition of hypoglycemia, or low blood sugar, that contributes to extreme or erratic swings in mood and behavior. When the brain is deprived of adequate glucose due to this condition, the higher rational centers are the first to shut down, leaving the person without a more balanced overview of his situation. Exaggerated emotional responses, sometimes approaching the point of panic, make it harder to find solutions to one's problems. Feelings of being trapped or stifled by a relationship, or in some cases, chronic depression about not being in a relationship, are also the product of this condition.

Impotence and Premature Ejaculation

Many women are unable to experience orgasm because of the inability of their partners. If a woman is married to a man who is impotent, who ejaculates prematurely, or who is selfish and thinks only of his needs, she is denied the opportunity to experience sexual fulfillment. For a woman in this situation, sexual experiences are often over before she has a chance to become fully aroused or to reach orgasm. When intercourse begins, she may try to hurry her response or force herself to have an orgasm, and this distraction prevents her from responding in a free and uninhibited way. If this happens often, she can easily develop feelings of anger and resentment toward her partner.

Men have the tendency to want to proceed directly to intercourse and orgasm. A healthy man is able to produce hundreds of millions of sperm every day. This creates the need for frequent sexual discharge. In contrast, only one ovum matures every twenty-eight days. If a man's urges are blocked or prevented, he feels frustrated. Men react to this in different ways. Some men become angry or violent, others seek sexual outlets elsewhere, while others become depressed or withdrawn.

Men's sexual energies begin at the center of the body. They discharge sperm outward from this center. Female sexuality is the opposite. It begins at the periphery of the body and culminates in the taking in or receiving of energy. If a man approaches a woman too forcefully or directly, without taking time to peripherally energize her, she can easily be turned off and withdraw. As we saw in the previous section, it is better to begin by energizing the periphery of the body and then continue by gradually spiraling inward toward the center. Light touching of the skin, especially along the meridian pathways of energy, is particularly exciting and pleasing to a woman. Strong touch to the extent that a woman feels hard pressure or pain can create unpleasant sensations that constrict the chakras and block the flow of energy through them. When a man applies light touch all over a woman's body, energy is fed to the centrally located chakras, causing them to become highly charged and her to become very aroused and stimulated.

Fatigue

Another common cause of the inability to achieve orgasm is an underlying condition of fatigue or exhaustion that results from the overintake of extremely yin foods and drinks, including sugar, chocolate, ice cream, chilled soft drinks, tropical fruits, and others. These foods deplete the body's reserves of energy and, in extreme cases, can trigger a condition such as **chronic fatique syndrome**, or CFS. People with this illness, sometimes called **chronic Epstein-Barr virus syndrome**, experience fatigue that impairs daily activity by 50 percent for at least six months, along with other symptoms of a weakened immune system such as swollen glands, low-grade fever, sore throat, aching joints, elevated white blood cell counts, painful lymph nodes, migraines, and others. Persons with this problem have unusually high antibody counts of Epstein-Barr virus, a member of the herpes virus family. About two million people in the United States are estimated to have CFS. The majority are in their thirties and forties. Obviously, a condition such as this depletes the body of the energy needed for active and satisfying sex.

Gynecological Disorders

A variety of gynecological disorders also interfere with a woman's enjoyment of sex. Fibroids, or fleshy growths within or on the wall of the uterus, block the smooth flow of heaven and earth's forces along the primary channel and diminish the energy received by the sexual organs. They consist of masses of fibrous tissue and may be single or multiple, large or small.

Fibroids are widespread today and result from an extreme diet, especially the overconsumption of foods containing cholesterol and saturated fat such as eggs, meat, dairy products, and poultry, in combination with extremely yin foods and beverages such as sugar, tropical fruits, oils, soft drinks, and chocolate. When these items are eaten regularly, mucus and fat begin to deposit in the body, initially in areas connected to the outside such as the sinuses, breasts, lungs, intestines, kidneys; and in the reproductive organs, such as in the ovaries, uterus, and Fallopian tubes or around the prostate gland in men.

Fats in the bloodstream can be deposited in the organs, contributing to the formation of cysts and tumors. When this occurs in the muscle of the uterus, the result is a fibroid. Fibroids often begin as small seedlings. Whether or not they enlarge depends on the quality and volume of fat and other forms of excess eaten by the woman. Frequently, they continue growing as the result of an improper diet, and begin to bulge either through the outer lining of the uterus or through the inner lining or endometrium. In some cases, they bulge so far that they are pushed out on a stalk.

Fibroids may or may not produce noticeable symptoms. The most common age for symptoms to occur is between thirty-five and forty-five, although women of all ages can experience them. A common symptom is bleeding, especially in the form of heavy and prolonged periods. This happens because fibroids frequently distort the uterus so that the surface area of the endometrium is increased. A greater amount of endometrial lining is thus produced each month, thereby increasing the menstrual flow. In this case, it is also more difficult for bleeding to stop since the normal spiral musculature of the uterine wall is distorted and cannot contract around the blood vessel. Fibroids may grow to become quite large, even to the size of a football, and may begin to cause pain as a result of pressing on other organs.

Ovarian cysts and tumors also interfere with a woman's sexuality and develop through a process similar to that in which fibroids appear. There are literally dozens of varieties of ovarian growths, and each is the result of a specific excess in the woman's diet.

The most common ovarian growth is the simple cyst that develops when the ovarian follicle does not rupture and release its egg but instead continues growing. These cysts are generally more yin and result from the overconsumption of milk, butter, and other light dairy products, soy milk or soy ice cream, sugar, animal fats, and oily and greasy foods.

Another common type of ovarian growth is the dermoid cyst. Dermoid cysts are often found in younger women and contain fat, hair, and calcified material. Dermoid cysts are more yang or "hard," and arise primarily from the overconsumption of hard, saturated fat such as that in eggs, meat, poultry, and cheese. Foods that deplete calcium from the bones, including refined sugar and nightshade vegetables such as tomatoes, potatoes, eggplant, and peppers, contribute to the formation of these cysts.

Vaginal infections also interfere with the enjoyment of sexuality. They can cause intercourse to be painful. As previously mentioned, the female sex organs are a frequent site for the accumulation of excess fat and mucus. These factors are commonly expelled through the vagina, producing a variety of vaginal discharges. When the localization of fat and mucus upsets the delicate biochemical balance in this region, especially the normal acidity of the vagina, a variety of organisms can begin to grow and cause vaginal infection.

These conditions are common when foods such as milk, butter, eggs, cheese, chicken, and others containing animal fat are eaten regularly, or when tropical fruits, sugar, soft drinks, and other extreme yin foods are consumed. Even women who eat a naturally balanced diet can develop vaginal discharges if too many fruits, nuts, flour products, soy milk, or chips or other oily foods are consumed.

Hip Bath and Douche

In traditional macrobiotic medicine, a hip bath is frequently used by women to help relieve reproductive disorders, including fibroids, cysts, and vaginal infections. To prepare a hip bath, run hot water in the bathtub and add several large handfuls of sea salt to the water. Use only enough water to cover the body from the waist down. Sit in the tub and cover your upper body with a thick cotton towel to prevent chills and absorb perspiration. If the bath water begins to cool, add more hot water and stay in the bath for ten to twelve minutes.

The hot bath will activate blood circulation in your lower body and your skin may turn red. This circulation will loosen deposits of fat and mucus in the pelvic region.

Following the hip bath, douche with a special solution. Prepare this either by squeezing the juice from half a lemon into warm bancha tea or water, or by adding one or two teaspoons of brown rice vinegar to bancha tea or warm water. Add a tiny, three-finger pinch of sea salt, stir, and use as a douche. The douching solution helps dislodge deposits of mucus and fat that have been loosened during the bath. The hip bath and douche can be repeated several times per week for four to six weeks. During this time, it is important to eat well and avoid foods that contribute to the buildup of excess in the reproductive tract. Some of these foods are cheese, ice cream, butter, sugary desserts, eggs, meat, and poultry. On the whole, avoid foods that contain saturated fat and cholesterol—foods of animal origin.

Monilial infections are a common cause for pain during intercourse (*Monilia* is a type of fungus). These infections produce a thick white discharge and cause the labia to become swollen, red, and itchy. They often make urination painful as well.

Another common vaginal infection produces a thinner and more yellow-colored discharge that contains a protozoan known as *Trichomonas vaginalis*. It can cause an itching sensation that seems to be centered inside the vagina, as well as pain and burning during intercourse. This infection is sexually transmittable.

In some cases, fat and mucus accumulate in the blood vessels that supply the vagina and just below the surface of the skin that lines the vagina. This can cause thinning of the vaginal walls and reduce the amount of lubrication secreted during sexual arousal. These conditions are a common cause of painful intercourse and result primarily from overconsumption of animal fats. Hormone imbalances, especially a reduction of estrogen, frequently accompany these conditions and are also the result of an unbalanced diet, especially the overintake of animal food. Accumulation of fat and mucus under the foreskin of the clitoris can also cause pain during intercourse, while endometriosis and infections in the cervix, uterus, and Fallopian tubes can also make intercourse unpleasant and painful. These conditions are accelerated by the intake of animal fats and other extremes in the diet.

Foods That Restore a Woman's Vitality

As we can see, a balanced natural diet is essential in dissolving the physical blockages that inhibit the flow of energy and interfere with the ability to respond sexually and to achieve orgasm. Dietary change in the direction of macrobiotics can also be used in the recovery from fibroids, ovarian cysts, vaginal infections, and other gynecological disorders.* It is best to avoid meat, eggs, chicken, cheese, milk, and other foods high in saturated fat and cholesterol. At the same time, chocolate, ice

---

*The macrobiotic approach to women's health, including recommendations for a variety of gynecological disorders, is presented in detail in the book *Infertility and Reproductive Disorders* (Japan Publications), by Michio Kushi.

cream, honey, refined sugar, carob, alcohol, tropical fruits, soft drinks, and drugs or medications—all of which weaken the flow of energy in the chakras—are best avoided.

Whole cereal grains provide a smooth, steady release of energy and can be eaten as principal foods. As with the other sexual problems discussed in this chapter, the intake of cookies, muffins, crackers, and other baked flour products is best kept to a minimum. This is important for women recovering from gynecological disorders, as flour products can cause mucus to develop in the body, even when whole grain flours are used. In cases where a woman's condition is overly tight, grains can be temporarily cooked with enough water to give them a soft, creamy consistency. Barley, a grain known for its light, expansive energy, can be helpful in melting deposits of hard fat caused by animal foods. Corn on the cob, fresh and in season, can also be eaten often to relax an overly tight condition (without butter, of course).

Soups can be included twice daily, as indicated in Chapter 2. Lightly seasoned miso soup can be eaten once a day, while other varieties such as barley/vegetable, rice/vegetable, other whole grain and vegetable soups, bean and vegetable soups, and sweet squash soup can be included as well.

Sea vegetables, such as wakame or kombu, are best included daily in soups, as the balanced minerals they contain help the body discharge fats and mucus and strengthen conductivity to energy. Daikon radish and shiitake mushrooms can also be cooked often in soups. They help dissolve fat deposits caused by animal foods and relax tightness and hardening in the body. Also, sweet-tasting vegetables such as squash, carrots, cabbage, and daikon can be cooked often in miso and other soups to help relieve the symptoms of hypoglycemia. Millet soup, cooked with either squash or carrots, or puréed squash soup can be especially helpful for this condition.

A wide variety of cooked vegetable dishes can be included daily. They can be cooked in many ways to guarantee a wide range of energies. Hard leafy greens, such as daikon, carrot, turnip, and radish tops, are especially helpful in melting fat deposits. Daikon radish can also be used for this purpose, and can be cooked together with its green top or eaten in its dried and shredded form. For someone lacking strength and vitality, root vegetables such as carrot, burdock, and lotus root can help restore energy. Also, for hypoglycemia, sweet-tasting vegetables can be included on a daily basis. They are delicious when cooked in a variety of dishes.

If a woman is experiencing a vaginal infection, cysts, or fibroids, or if she lacks energy and vitality, it is better to minimize the intake of raw salad. Quickly steamed greens or lightly blanched vegetables can be eaten daily to satisfy salad cravings. It is also better for those who have eaten plenty of animal fat or oily, greasy foods to temporarily limit their intake of oil. A small amount of high-quality sesame or corn oil can be used several times per week in making occasional sautéed vegetables or fried rice. It is also better to emphasize low-fat beans, such as azuki beans, chickpeas, lentils, and black soybeans, and to use the other varieties only on occasion until one's condition improves. However, soybean products such as tofu, dried tofu, and tempeh may be used regularly.

Sea vegetable side dishes are also important, since, as we have seen, minerals help the body to discharge fats, mucus, and other toxins. Besides using sea vegetables in soups or in cooking beans, vegetables, and other dishes, varieties such as arame and hijiki can be eaten in small side dishes on a regular basis, several times per week. Sea vegetable condiments, such as roasted and crushed kombu or wakame powders, are also fine for regular use, along with gomashio and other condiments recommended in Chapter 2.

It is better to minimize the use of fruit during the recovery process, limiting intake to a small volume of cooked or dried temperate climate fruits only on occasion. The intake of raw fruits and fruit juices is also best minimized, especially by those with chronic fatigue or weakness (such as that in Chronic Fatigue Syndrome—CFS) or with gynecological disorders. Nuts and nut butters, which contain plenty of fat and oil, are also best avoided until recovery is complete. Chestnuts, however, are an exception because of the lower fat content and the high quality of complex carbohydrate they contain. They can be used on occasion to add sweetness to various dishes. Also, a small amount of rice syrup, barley malt, amazake, or other high-quality grain sweetener may be used from time to time to add a sweet flavor. Lightly roasted seeds, including sesame and pumpkin seeds, can be used as snacks, together with others listed in Chapter 2.

It is best to limit the intake of animal foods, although low-fat white meat fish can be eaten on occasion, on average about once or twice per week. Persons suffering from fatigue, exhaustion, or CFS may also use the carp-burdock soup (Vitality Stew) presented earlier in this chapter to help restore strength.

In general, beverages, seasonings, condiments, and pickles can be used according to the guidelines in Chapter 2.

Home health care practices, such as daily body scrubbing with a hot moist towel and the hip bath and douche described above, can also be helpful in restoring vitality and helping the body dissolve fats and other forms of excess. Other way-of-life practices mentioned at the beginning of this chapter are also recommended for optimal health and vitality, including chewing well, not eating before bed, cooking foods on a gas stove, exercising regularly, and wearing natural fabrics. The sweet vegetable drink described in Chapter 2 is especially recommended for those suffering from the extreme mood swings, including depression, that are due to hypoglycemia.

As hardened deposits of fat and mucus are discharged, the body will become softer, more flexible, and alive. The energies of heaven and earth will stream freely through the chakras and meridians, charging and invigorating them with life energy. As vibrant health is restored, the experience of sex will become fulfilling and rewarding.

The release of physical hardness and rigidity makes it easier to let go of negative emotions such as guilt, fear, anger, and resentment. Daily body scrubbing is especially helpful in releasing this stagnated energy, as is regular exercise and sweet vegetable drink.

Medications, including antibiotics, aspirin, birth control pills, and other prescription and over-the-counter drugs, further weaken the charge of energy in the chakras and throughout the body. And as we saw earlier, tonsillectomies, abortions, and other common surgical procedures also diminish sexual vitality.

Expectations About Your Partner

Frustration often arises in relationships when fixed expectations about a partner exist. Often, an image is created of how the partner should be, and the person with the image tries to fit him or her into that mold. Soon these expectations harden into unwritten laws. Then, if one's partner does something unexpected or doesn't conform to these expectations, the other feels angry, let down, and frustrated.

Life does not conform to fixed or rigid rules. It is far too dynamic, flexible, and changing. Disappointment over unfulfilled expectations occurs when our physical and mental conditions become hard and inflexible due to overintake of foods that contain saturated fat and cholesterol. However, as we change our diets and conditions, the increased flexibility in body and mind that follows makes it much easier to become loving and accepting and to change negative feelings into their opposites. Giving and receiving massages on a regular basis can be very helpful in releasing emotional and physical blockages and stagnation. It can be done as often as needed as a part of a healthful lifestyle.

The ideal situation is when both partners in a relationship help each other eat and live in a healthful way. As they continue together, they will experience more complete love and harmony, together with the freedom to explore their sexuality without fear or hesitation. By loving each other, they can discover a love for all of humanity and nature. The joy that comes from the harmonious union of yin and yang will permeate every aspect of their existence. Through love and sexuality, they can come to discover the endless love and harmony of the universe.

5.

Recipes for Healthy Sexuality

Food has a powerful influence on sexuality. A happy and healthy sex life begins in the kitchen. Selecting the highest quality foods and preparing them properly are both important for sexual happiness throughout life.

The guidelines of macrobiotics have been practiced by hundreds of thousands of people throughout the world, including many couples and families. A similar way of eating has been generally observed by many cultures until the twentieth century. In contrast to the modern high-fat, low-fiber diet, macrobiotics is based on the following nutritional considerations.

- A higher consumption of balanced complex carbohydrates and a reduced intake of extremely expansive simple sugars.

- A greater use of protein from more balanced whole grains, beans, and other vegetable foods and a lesser use of proteins derived from extremely contractive animal foods.

- A lower intake of fat with an increased use of unsaturated fats and oils and a decreased use of saturated fat.

- An adequate consideration of the ideal balance among vitamins, minerals, and other nutrients.

- The use of more organically grown and unprocessed foods and fewer chemically sprayed or fertilized items.

- The use of more traditionally processed foods and fewer artificially and chemically processed foods.

- An increase in the intake of foods in the whole form and less use of refined or partial foods such as white rice, white bread, and others.

- The greater use of foods rich in natural fiber and less use of foods that have been devitalized.

Eating this way reduces the risk of heart disease, high blood pressure, diet-related cancers, and other chronic illnesses associated with the modern diet. It helps us avoid many of the foods that are high in the saturated fat and cholesterol that block the smooth flow of energy in the body. As we saw in the previous chapter, accumulations of fat and cholesterol create energy blockages in the body that impede sensitivity and sexual ability. The complex carbohydrates and other essential nutrients in whole grains, beans, vegetables, and sea vegetables provide a smooth, steady source of energy that contributes to sexual vitality, endurance, and sensitivity.

The foods in the standard macrobiotic diet can be divided into primary and supplementary categories. The primary category consists of foods eaten daily—whole grains, beans, vegetables, and sea vegetables—while the supplementary category includes foods eaten either several times a week, such as low-fat white meat fish and local fruits in season, or those such as condiments, beverages, seasonings, and pickles that are consumed daily but in much smaller quantities than primary foods. The proportions in the standard macrobiotic diet are ideal in a temperate or four-season climate. They require some adjustment if you live a different climate. People in the far northern or Arctic regions, for example, need a larger volume of animal protein and fat, while those in equatorial zones can get by with much less.

The percentages of foods listed below are based on the overall amount of food consumed each day and are calculated by approximate volume and not by weight. It isn't necessary to include foods from each major category every time you eat, though whole cereal grains are recommended at each meal.

The number and variety of side dishes you prepare to complement your grain dishes depends on your appetite, preferences, and time available for cooking.

WHOLE CEREAL GRAINS

Whole cereal grains are the staff of life and are an essential part of a way of eating for healthy sexuality. For people in temperate climates, they may comprise up to 50 to 60 percent of daily intake. Refer to Table 5.1 for a list of the whole grains and grain products that may be included.

Brown Rice

Brown rice is rice that has not been polished and therefore contains optimal fiber and nutrients. We recommend that you use organic brown rice—rice that has been grown without chemical pesticides or fertilizers.

Table 5.1. Whole Grains and Grain Products

For Regular Use	For Occasional Use	Flour Products for Occasional Use
Barley	Corn grits	Fu
Buckwheat	Corn meal	Seitan
Corn	Couscous	Soba (buckwheat) noodles
Medium grain brown rice (in warmer areas or seasons)	Cracked wheat (bulghur)	Somen (thin wheat) noodles
Millet	Long grain brown rice	Udon (wheat) noodles
Pearl barley (hatto mugi)	Mochi (pounded sweet rice)	Unyeasted whole rye bread
Rye	Rolled oats	Unyeasted whole wheat bread
Short grain brown rice	Rye flakes	Whole wheat noodles
Whole oats	Steel cut oats	
Whole wheat berries	Sweet brown rice	
Other traditionally used whole grains	Other traditionally used whole grain products	

Grains, beans, vegetables, sea vegetables, and fruits sometimes have soil or small stones mixed in with them, and this is perfectly natural. These foods need to be washed before you cook with them. To wash brown rice or other grains, place them, a handful at a time, on a plate. Look for small stones, bits of soil, or broken or discolored grains. Sort and remove these. Then place the grains in a bowl or cooking pot, put it in the sink, and add enough cold water to cover. Stir the grains gently with your fingers. Pour the water off and repeat the procedure. Place the grains in a strainer and rinse quickly, but thoroughly, under a stream of cold water. This helps remove minute particles of dust that may still be attached to the grains. Your grains are now ready to be cooked. Once they have been washed, do not let them sit for too long before you cook them, as this will cause them to absorb the water and lose freshness.

Pressure cooking is the preferred method of cooking brown rice the majority of the time. Pressure cooking allows the rice to cook thoroughly. Pressure-cooked rice is more easily digested, retains more nutrients, is a little less soggy, and has stronger energy than rice cooked by other methods. There are several ways to pressure cook brown rice. The following are two of the most often used methods.

Nonsoaking. Place the brown rice in a pressure cooker and add the appropriate measure of water. (The usual measurement is 1.5 parts water to 1 part brown rice.) Do not cover. Place on a low flame for approximately 10 minutes. This is a presoaking period, which allows the grain to slowly expand, making it more digestible and sweet. Add the appropriate amount of sea salt (one pinch per cup), cover, and turn the flame to high. Bring to pressure. When the pressure is up, reduce the flame to medium-low and place a flame deflector under the cooker. Pressure cook for 50 minutes, remove from the cooker, and serve.

Soaking. Place the brown rice and water in a pressure cooker and soak overnight or for 6-8 hours. Add the appropriate amount of sea salt after the grain has soaked. Cover, place on a high flame, and bring up to pressure. When the pressure is up, reduce the flame to medium-low and cook for 50 minutes.

Basic Pressure-Cooked Brown Rice
---

2 cups organic brown rice, washed
2 1/2–3 cups water
Pinch of sea salt per cup of grain

Pressure cook using one of the methods described on page 128. Remove the pressure cooker from the flame and allow the pressure to come down naturally. Remove the cover and allow the rice to sit for 4-5 minutes. Remove the rice and place in a wooden serving bowl.

Brown Rice with Pearl Barley
---

1 1/2 cups organic brown rice, washed
1/2 cup pearl barley (hato mugi), washed
  and soaked 4-6 hours
2 1/2-3 cups water
Pinch of sea salt per cup of grain

Pressure cook using one of the methods described on page 128. Remove the pressure cooker from the flame and allow the pressure to come down naturally. Remove the cover and allow the rice to sit for 4–5 minutes. Remove the rice and place in a wooden serving bowl.

Brown Rice with Millet
---

1 1/2 cups organic brown rice, washed
1/2 cup millet, washed
3 cups water
Pinch of sea salt per cup of grain

Pressure cook using one of the methods described on page 128. Remove the pressure cooker from the flame and allow the pressure to come down naturally. Remove the cover and allow the rice to sit for 4–5 minutes. Remove the rice and millet and place in a wooden serving bowl.

Boiled Brown Rice

> 2 cups organic brown rice, washed
> 4 cups water
> Pinch of sea salt per cup of grain

Place the rice, water, and sea salt in a heavy cooking pot. Cover and bring to a boil. Reduce the flame to medium-low and simmer for about 1 hour or until all the water has been absorbed. Remove and place in a wooden serving bowl.

Boiled rice can also be cooked using any of the variations listed for pressure-cooked rice.

Rice Triangles (Musubi)

These ingredients will make one rice ball. To make more, simply use more rice, nori, and umeboshi. Rice balls are a great way to use leftover rice.

> 1 cup cooked short grain brown rice
> 1/2 sheet toasted nori, cut in half
> 1/2-1 umeboshi plum
> Pinch of sea salt

Dampen your hands slightly in a small bowl of water with the pinch of sea salt in it. Place the rice in your hands and form into a triangular shape by cupping your hands into a "V" and applying pressure to mold the rice. The triangle should be firmly packed. With your index finger, poke a hole into the center of the rice and insert the umeboshi plum. Then close the hole by packing the triangle firmly again. Place 1 square of the toasted nori on one side of the triangle and the other square on the other side. Pack the rice triangle again so that the nori sticks to it. You may occasionally need to dampen your hands with a very small amount of the salted water to prevent rice and nori from sticking to them. If there are uncovered spots on the triangle, you can patch them by sticking small pieces of toasted nori on them until the triangle is completely covered with nori.

Soft Rice
---

1 cup organic brown rice, washed
5 cups water
Pinch of sea salt

Place all ingredients in a pressure cooker and cover. Bring to pressure, reduce the flame to medium-low, and cook for 50-55 minutes. Serve with umeboshi and roasted nori strips or your favorite condiment and scallions.

Fried Rice

1-2 tablespoons dark sesame oil
1/2 cup diced celery
1 diced onion
1 tablespoon minced scallion
1/2 cup carrot, sliced in thin matchsticks
1/2 cup burdock, sliced in thin matchsticks
1-2 tablespoons water (if the rice is dry)
2 cups cooked brown rice
1 tablespoon chopped parsley or scallion for garnish
Tamari soy sauce or sea salt

Place the oil in a skillet and heat up. Add the scallion and sauté 1 minute. Next, place the onion and celery in the skillet and sauté 1-2 minutes. Add the carrot and burdock. Place the rice on top of the vegetables, and if the rice is dry, add water. Cover the skillet and reduce the flame to low. Simmer for 15-20 minutes or until the vegetables are soft and the rice is warm. Just before the vegetables and rice are done, add the tamari soy sauce to taste or add a small amount of sea salt for a mild salt taste. Add the chopped parsley or scallions, cover, and cook another 2-3 minutes. Mix all the ingredients together and serve hot.

Brown Rice and Beans

Brown rice is delicious when cooked with beans such as azuki, chickpeas, black soybeans, and others. Like whole grains, beans are purchased dried. Listed below are several ways brown rice and beans can be prepared.

- *Boil* the beans with water to cover for 20 minutes. Add to the rice along with the remaining cooking water and sea salt (use a pinch of salt per cup of beans). Cook as for plain brown rice. This method can be used often with azuki beans.

- *Soak* the beans 6-8 hours or overnight. Discard the soaking water and add the beans to the rice along with water and sea salt. Then pressure cook as you would plain brown rice.

- *Dry roast* the beans. This method is used only with white or black soybeans. Wash the beans and dry roast several minutes on a medium flame, stirring constantly. You can tell the beans are done when the skin becomes very tight and splits in half. Add the beans to the rice, along with water and sea salt. Pressure cook as for plain brown rice.

When combining beans with rice, the percentage of beans is usually kept between 10-20 percent with the exception of azuki beans, which can make up as much as 30 percent of the dish.

The soaking water from azuki beans can be included as part of the water measurement in cooking. The soaking water from other beans is usually discarded when cooking them with rice.

Black Bean Rice

---

1 1/2 cups organic brown rice, washed
1/2 cup black soybeans, washed
1 1/2–2 cups water
Pinch of sea salt per cup of grain and
    beans

Place a stainless steel skillet on a medium flame and heat up. Place the washed black soybeans in the skillet. Dry roast, stirring constantly to prevent burning, until the skin of the beans becomes tight and splits open slightly.

Place the rice and roasted black soybeans in a pressure cooker. Add the water and cook using one of the methods described on page 128. When the rice is done, remove the cooker from the burner and allow the pressure to come down. Remove the cover and allow the rice to sit 4-5 minutes before removing, and place in a wooden serving bowl.

Sweet Rice with Chestnuts

---

1 1/2 cups organic brown rice, washed
1/2 cup dried chestnuts, washed
2 1/2-3 cups water
Pinch of sea salt per cup of grain and
    chestnuts

Take a stainless steel skillet, place it on a medium flame, and heat up. Place the damp chestnuts in the heated skillet. Dry roast several minutes, stirring constantly back and forth with a wooden spoon until the chestnuts are a golden brown, but not burnt.

Place the rice, roasted chestnuts, and water in a pressure cooker and cook using one of the methods described on page

128. When the rice and chestnuts are done, remove them from the burner and allow the pressure to come down. Remove the cover and allow the rice to sit for 4-5 minutes before placing in a wooden serving bowl.

Sweet rice is a more glutenous variety of brown rice that is rich in protein. It is used less often than regular brown rice and may be included several times per week. It can be served plain, cooked with a variety of ingredients, or pounded and made into mochi.

Mochi (Pounded Sweet Rice)

Mochi is cooked sweet rice that has been pounded with a wooden pestle for 30-40 minutes or more until it becomes sticky. It is then dried for 2-3 days.

Mochi can be purchased prepackaged in most natural foods stores. To serve, cut into small squares and dry roast in a skillet until it is slightly browned on both sides and puffs up slightly.

Mochi may also be steamed, baked, broiled, pan-fried in oil, deep-fried, or added to soups and stews. Mochi may be eaten with a variety of toppings, including tamari soy sauce, warm brown rice syrup, or toasted soybean flour (kinako). Mochi can also be dry roasted or toasted and placed in miso soup.

Recipes for making homemade mochi are included in the cookbooks listed on page 193.

Corn

There are several varieties of soft and hard corn available in natural foods stores. Sweet corn is available in many varieties ranging in color from yellow to white. It can be eaten as corn on the cob and, because it is perishable, is usually eaten in season. Hard corn can be used as a whole grain and, because it is dried, can be stored for long periods, making it available in any season. Several types of hard, dried corn are available.

Hard, dried varieties of corn are traditionally cooked with pure wood ashes, which help soften the hard shell and add calcium and other minerals to the corn.

Whole Corn
---

2 cups whole dried corn, washed and
    soaked overnight (preferably dent corn)
2 cups pure sifted wood ash, tied in a clean
    cotton muslin bag or sack
4 cups water
Pinch of sea salt

Place the corn in a pressure cooker. Add the wood ash and two cups of water. Cover and pressure cook for 1-1 1/2 hours. Remove from the flame and allow the pressure to come down. Remove the cover and place the corn in a strainer or colander. Rinse all of the wood ashes from the corn. Place the corn into a clean pressure cooker, add sea salt, and pressure cook for 1 more hour. Remove from the flame, allow the pressure to come down, and place the cooked corn in a serving dish or use in making soups, vegetable dishes, or salads.

Other Grains

Boiled Barley
---

2 cups barley, soaked 6-8 hours
4-5 cups water
Pinch of sea salt per cup of
    barley

Place the soaked barley in a heavy stainless steel pot. Add the water and sea salt. Cover the pot, place on a high flame, and bring to a boil. Reduce the flame to medium-low and simmer for 1 1/2 hours. Remove from the flame and spoon into a wooden serving bowl.

Variations. Barley may be boiled or pressure cooked with a variety of other grains, beans, and vegetables. Cook same as for plain brown rice. For soft barley cereal, add 4-5 cups of water to 1 cup of barley and pressure cook for about 1-1 1/4 hours. Serve hot and garnish with chopped scallions, parsley, toasted nori, gomashio, or your favorite condiment.

Boiled Millet and Vegetables

---

2 cups millet, washed
3-3 1/2 cups boiling water
1 cup hard winter squash, such as but-
    tercup, butternut, or Hokkaido
    pumpkin, cut in 1-inch chunks
1/2 cup carrots, sliced in chunks
1/4 cup cabbage, sliced in 1-inch
    squares
Pinch of sea salt per cup of millet

Place all ingredients in a heavy pot, cover and bring to a boil. Reduce the flame to medium-low and cook for about 30-35 minutes. Remove from the flame. Remove the cover and place the millet in a wooden serving bowl. Garnish and serve.

Variations. Dry roast millet until golden yellow and combine with vegetables and cook as above. Millet may be pressure cooked with vegetables using about 1 1/2 cups of water per cup of millet. Cook for 15-20 minutes on a medium-low flame. For soft millet cereal, cook with 5 cups of water per cup of millet and either boil for 30-35 minutes or pressure cook for 15-20 minutes. Millet can also be used in making soups and stews.

Buckwheat (Kasha)

---

1 cup buckwheat groats, washed
2 cups boiling water
Pinch of sea salt

Dry roast the washed buckwheat for about 5 minutes, stirring constantly. Place the sea salt and buckwheat in boiling water.

Cover and reduce the flame to medium-low. Simmer for 20-30 minutes or until the buckwheat is soft and all the water has been absorbed. Remove and place in a serving bowl. Garnish and serve.

Fried Udon or Soba

---

6 cups water
1 eight-ounce package udon or
   soba
1 tablespoon dark sesame oil
1/2 cup onion, sliced in thin half-
   moons
1 cup shredded cabbage
1/2 cup carrots, sliced in thin
   matchsticks
1/4 cup sliced scallions
Tamari soy sauce

Place the water in a pot and bring to a boil. Add the udon or soba and stir once or twice to prevent them from sticking. Return to a boil. Reduce the flame to medium-high and cook several minutes until the noodles are the same color inside as outside. If the inside or center of the noodle is white or lighter in color than the outside, then cook a little longer. When done, place the noodles in a strainer or colander and rinse thoroughly under cold water to stop the cooking action and to prevent the noodles from sticking together in clumps. Set the noodles aside and allow to drain. They are now ready to use.

Brush dark sesame oil in a skillet and heat up. Add the onion and sauté 1-2 minutes. Layer the cabbage and carrots on top of the onion. Place the noodles on top of the vegetables, cover, and cook on a low flame for 5-7 minutes until the vegetables are tender and the noodles are hot. Add the scallions and a small amount of tamari soy sauce for a mild salt taste, cover, and continue to cook 1-2 minutes until the scallions are done. Mix and place in a serving bowl.

Udon with Vegetables and Kuzu Sauce
---

1 eight-ounce package udon, cooked
3 shiitake mushrooms, soaked and sliced
1/2 cup onion, sliced in 1/4-inch-thick
    wedges
1/2 cup carrots, sliced on a thin diagonal
1/4 cup celery, sliced on a thin diagonal
1 cup broccoli, sliced in small florets
1 cup tofu, cubed and pan-fried until
    golden
1 soaked strip kombu, 3-4 inches long
2 1/2 cups water
3 tablespoons kuzu, diluted in 3 table-
    spoons of water
1 1/2-2 tablespoons tamari soy sauce
Grated ginger for garnish (optional)
Sliced scallions for garnish

Remove the stems from the shiitake mushrooms. Place the water, shiitake, and kombu in a pot and bring to a boil. Cover and simmer 4-5 minutes. Remove the kombu and set aside for future use. Continue to cook the shiitake for another 5-7 minutes. Add the onion, carrots, celery, tofu, and broccoli. Cover, reduce the flame to medium, and simmer until the vegetables are tender but still slightly crisp and brightly colored.

Reduce the flame to low and add the diluted kuzu, stirring constantly to prevent lumping. When thick, add the tamari soy sauce for a mild salt taste and simmer 2-3 minutes. Place the cooked noodles in individual serving bowls and pour the vegetable-kuzu sauce over them. Garnish with a dab of fresh grated ginger and a few sliced scallions and serve hot.

Whole Wheat Products

Whole wheat flour is unprocessed and unbleached and therefore has many more essential nutrients than does white flour. The following recipes use whole wheat flour.

Whole Wheat Sourdough Bread

There are many types of unyeasted whole wheat sourdough breads available in most natural foods stores that can be used for occasional enjoyment. Whole wheat bread can be eaten plain, with various natural spreads, occasionally toasted, or steamed (which makes it moister and easier to digest). Recipes for making whole wheat sourdough bread at home are presented in the macrobiotic cookbooks listed at the end of this chapter.

Onion, carrot, squash, or sesame butter can be used as spreads on occasion.

Fu (Puffed Wheat Gluten)

Fu is made from the gluten of whole wheat flour and is naturally rich in protein. It is available prepackaged in most natural foods stores and comes in rounds or thin flat sheets. Fu can be used in soups, vegetable dishes, fried, and in some bean dishes. It is a dried flour product that must be soaked to reconstitute. After soaking for 5-10 minutes, simply slice and use. Because it is a moist, more easily digested product, fu can be eaten a little more often than hard baked flour products.

Fu and Vegetables

---

1 package round-shaped fu, soaked and
   sliced
1 cup chopped broccoli
1/4 cup green cabbage, sliced in 1-inch
   squares
1/2 cup carrots, sliced on a diagonal
1 cup fresh green peas
Pinch of sea salt
Water
Tamari soy sauce

Place the fu and vegetables in a pot. Add enough water to half-cover the ingredients. Place the cover on the pot and add a pinch of sea salt. Bring to a boil. Reduce the flame to medium-low and simmer for 10-15 minutes. Season mildly with several drops of tamari soy sauce. Cover and simmer for another 3-4 minutes. Remove and place in a serving bowl.

Seitan (Wheat Gluten)

Seitan is made from the gluten of whole wheat flour, but unlike fu it is not dried. It is also high in protein (it is sometimes called "wheat-meat"), and is more chewy than fu. Seitan can be purchased prepackaged in most natural foods stores or can be made at home.

Seitan and Onions

---

1 pound seitan, sliced
1 large Spanish onion, sliced in 1/4-inch-
    thick rings
1/2 cup water
1/2 cup chopped chives or scallions
Dark sesame oil

Brush a small amount of dark sesame oil on the bottom of a stainless steel skillet. Heat up the oil. Add the onion rings and sauté for 3-4 minutes. Place the sliced seitan on top of the onion rings. Do not mix. Add the water, cover, and bring to a boil. Reduce the flame to medium-low and cook for 15-20 minutes or until the onions are soft. Place the chopped chives or scallions on top of the seitan, cover, and simmer for another 1-2 minutes. Mix the ingredients and place in a serving bowl.

SOUP

Soups may comprise about 5-10 percent of each person's daily intake. For most people, that averages out to about one or two cups or bowls of soup per day, depending on their desires and preferences. Soups can include vegetables, grains, beans, sea vegetables, noodles or other grain products, bean products like tofu, tempeh, or others, and, occasionally, fish or seafood. Soups can be moderately seasoned with either miso, tamari soy sauce, sea salt, umeboshi plum or paste, or occasional ginger.

Light miso soup with vegetables and sea vegetables is recommended for daily consumption, on average one small bowl or cup per day. Mugi (barley) miso is recommended for regular consumption, followed by soybean (hatcho) miso. A second bowl or cup of soup may also be enjoyed, preferably seasoned mildly with tamari soy sauce or sea salt. Other soup varieties include bean and vegetable soups, grain and vegetable soups, and puréed squash and other vegetable soups.

Basic Vegetable-Miso Soup

4-5 cups water
1/2 cup wakame, washed, soaked, and
    sliced
2 cups onion, sliced in thin half-moons
3-4 teaspoons puréed barley or soybean
    (hatcho) miso
Sliced scallions for garnish

Place the water in a pot and bring to a boil. Add the wakame, reduce the flame to medium-low, cover, and simmer for 3-4 minutes. Add the onion, cover, and simmer another 2-4 minutes until the onion and wakame are tender. Reduce the flame to very low and add the puréed miso. Simmer another 2-3 minutes. Place in individual serving bowls and garnish with a few sliced scallions. Serve hot.

Kombu may be substituted for wakame. Simply soak for 3-4 minutes, slice in very thin matchsticks, and simmer for 5-10 minutes before adding the vegetables; or leave whole, simmer for 3-5 minutes, and remove.

Variations. The following combinations of vegetables can be used in Basic Vegetable-Miso Soup.

- Carrot, onion, cabbage, and wakame or kombu
- Daikon and wakame or kombu
- Daikon, shiitake, and wakame or kombu
- Daikon, celery, wakame or kombu, and parsley garnish
- Squash, onion, and wakame or kombu
- Celery, onion, scallion, and toasted nori garnish
- Carrot, onion, wakame or kombu, and tofu cubes
- Onion, shiitake, kombu, and parsley garnish
- Turnip, carrot, and wakame or kombu
- Wakame, onion, and toasted mochi
- Sweet corn, onion, and wakame or kombu

These are only a few of the variety of miso soups that can be created using different combinations of vegetables. Please experiment or refer to cookbooks for ideas.

Miso Soup with Brown Rice and Daikon

---

2 cups cooked brown rice
4-5 cups water
1/4 cup wakame or kombu, washed,
    soaked, and sliced
1/2 daikon, sliced in thin half-moons
1 cup sliced scallion
3 teaspoons puréed barley or soybean
    (hatcho) miso
Sliced scallions for garnish

Place the water in a pot and bring to a boil. Add the wakame or kombu, cover, and simmer for 3-4 minutes. Add the daikon, scallion, and cooked rice. Cover, reduce the flame to medium-low, and simmer about 10-15 minutes. Reduce the flame to very low and add the puréed miso and scallions. Cover and simmer 2-3 minutes. Place in individual serving bowls.

Udon or Soba with Tamari Soy Sauce Broth
---

1 eight-ounce package udon or soba,
    cooked, rinsed, and drained
4-5 cups water
1 strip kombu, 3 inches long, washed and
    soaked
2-3 soaked shiitake mushrooms
2 1/2-3 1/2 tablespoons tamari soy sauce
1/4 cup sliced scallions for garnish

Place the kombu, shiitake, and water in a pot. Bring to a boil. Cover and reduce the flame to medium-low. Simmer the kombu for 3-5 minutes and then remove, setting it aside for future use in other dishes. Simmer the shiitake for another 5-7 minutes and set aside for future use. Reduce the flame to low and add the tamari soy sauce. Simmer for 2-3 minutes. Place the cooked noodles in individual serving bowls and ladle the hot tamari broth over them. Garnish with sliced scallions and serve hot.

Variations. The shiitake mushrooms are an optional item in this recipe. You may use kombu only to prepare the stock.

Other vegetables may be added to the broth and simmered until tender after removing the kombu and shiitake. Then season with tamari soy sauce. Fresh tofu, dried tofu, tempeh, seitan, or even fu may also be used for variety. Also, instead of removing the kombu and shiitake mushrooms, they may be sliced very thin and left in the broth to be eaten with the noodles.

Azuki Bean Soup
---

1 cup azuki beans, washed and soaked 6-8
    hours
1 strip kombu, 1 inch long, soaked and
    diced

4-5 cups water (the bean soaking water
   may be used as part of this
   measurement)
1 cup cubed buttercup squash
1/2 cup sliced onion
1/4 cup carrots, sliced in chunks
1/4 cup celery, sliced in thick diagonals
1/4-1/2 teaspoon sea salt
Tamari soy sauce (optional)
Sliced scallions or chopped parsley for
   garnish

Place the kombu in a pot. Add the onion, celery, squash, and carrots. Place the azuki beans on top. Add the water, cover, and bring to a boil. Reduce the flame to medium-low and simmer until tender. Add the sea salt and continue to simmer until completely soft, which may take another 20-25 minutes. You may add several drops of tamari soy sauce just before serving for a slightly different flavor, but it is not necessary. Garnish and serve.

Lentil Soup

---

1 cup green lentils, washed
1 strip kombu, 4-5 inches long, washed,
   soaked, and diced
1/2 cup diced onion
1/2 cup diced carrots
1/4 cup diced celery
2 tablespoons diced burdock
1 cup whole wheat elbow pasta, cooked,
   rinsed, and drained
1/4 cup chopped parsley
4-5 cups water
1/4-1/2 teaspoon sea salt
Tamari soy sauce to taste (optional)

Place the kombu, onion, celery, carrots, and burdock in the pot. Set the lentils on top. Add the water, cover, and bring to a boil. Reduce the flame to medium-low. When the vegetables are tender, add the sea salt and cook another 20 minutes. Add the cooked pasta and the chopped parsley. Cook another 5 minutes or so. You may add a little tamari soy sauce for a mild salt taste, if desired, at the same time you add the pasta.

Soybean Stew

---

1 cup white soybeans, washed and soaked 6-8 hours
1 strip kombu, 3-4 inches long, washed, soaked, and diced
2 shiitake mushrooms, stems removed, soaked and diced
1/4 cup dried daikon, washed, soaked, and sliced
1/4 cup dried tofu, soaked, and cubed
1/4 cup diced celery
1/2 cup diced carrots
2 tablespoons diced burdock
3 tablespoons fresh or dried lotus root, soaked
1/2 cup cooked seitan
3 cups water
Grated ginger for garnish
Tamari soy sauce to taste
Sliced scallions for garnish

Place the kombu in a pressure cooker. Add the beans and water. Cover and bring up to pressure. Reduce the flame to medium-low and cook for 30 minutes. Remove from the flame and allow the pressure to come down. Remove the cover and add the shiitake, dried daikon, dried tofu, celery, carrots, burdock, lotus root, and seitan. Place the cover back on the pressure cooker and bring up to pressure again. Reduce the flame to medium-low and simmer another 20-25 minutes. Remove from the flame and allow the pressure to come down. Remove the cover, add a small amount of tamari soy sauce for a mild salt taste, and simmer another 3-4 minutes. Place in individual serving bowls and garnish with a dab of grated ginger and a few sliced scallions.

Millet Squash Soup

1/2 cup millet, washed and dry roasted
    until golden yellow
4-5 cups water
1 strip kombu, 1 inch long, soaked and
    diced
1 cup cubed butternut squash
1/2 cup diced onion
1/4 cup diced celery
1/2 cup cauliflower florets
1/4-1/2 teaspoon sea salt
Sliced scallions for garnish
Toasted nori strips for garnish

Layer ingredients in a pot in the following order: kombu, celery, onion, cauliflower, squash, and finally millet on top of the vegetables. Add a small pinch of sea salt and enough water to just cover the millet. Cover and bring to a boil. Reduce the flame to low and simmer until the millet is soft. This may take about 30 minutes. Occasionally during cooking you may need to add water, as the millet expands and absorbs water. Add only enough to just cover the millet each time until the millet is done. When done, you may add a little more water for the desired thickness you choose, and add the remaining sea salt. Cover and continue to cook another 10 minutes or so. Place in individual serving bowls, garnish, and serve.

Millet and Corn Soup

1/2 cup millet, washed
1 cup sweet corn, removed from cob
1/2 cup diced onion
1/4 cup diced celery
4-5 cups water
1/4-1/2 teaspoon sea salt
1/4 cup chopped parsley

Place a stainless steel skillet on a medium-high flame and heat up. Add the millet and dry roast until golden yellow. Place the onions, celery, sweet corn, and millet in a pot. Add the water and a pinch of sea salt. Cover and bring to a boil. Reduce the flame to medium-low and simmer for 30-35 minutes. Add the remaining sea salt, cover, and simmer for another 10 minutes. Place in individual serving bowls and garnish each bowl with a teaspoon of chopped parsley.

Pearl Barley (Hato Mugi) Soup

1/2 cup pearl barley (hato mugi), washed
    and soaked 4-6 hours
1 strip kombu, 3-4 inches long, soaked and
    diced
1/2 cup diced onion
1/2 cup diced carrots
1/4 cup diced celery
1/4 cup dried daikon, washed, soaked, and
    chopped
1/4 cup shiitake mushrooms, soaked and
    diced
2 tablespoons chopped scallions for
    garnish
4-5 cups water
1/4-1/2 teaspoon sea salt

Place the kombu in a pot. Add the shiitake, onion, celery, carrots, dried daikon, and pearl barley layers on top of the kombu in the order given above. Add the water and a pinch of sea salt. Cover and bring to a boil. Reduce the flame to medium-low and simmer for about 30-40 minutes. Add the remaining sea salt, cover, and simmer for another 10-15 minutes. Remove and place in individual serving bowls. Garnish each bowl with chopped scallions and serve hot.

Buckwheat Soup

1/2 cup dry roasted buckwheat
4-5 cups water
1 cup diced onion
1/2 cup diced celery
1/4 cup minced parsley
Pinch of sea salt
Tamari soy sauce

Place the buckwheat in a pot. Add the onion, celery, water, and sea salt. Cover and bring to a boil. Reduce the flame to medium-low and simmer for about 15-20 minutes. Season with a small amount of sea salt for a mild salt taste and add the minced parsley. Reduce the flame to low and simmer for another 4-5 minutes. Serve hot.

Puréed Squash Soup

---

4 cups cubed buttercup squash or
    Hokkaido pumpkin, washed, skin and
    seeds removed
4-5 cups water
1/4-1/2 teaspoon sea salt
Sliced scallions or chopped parsley for
    garnish
Toasted nori strips for garnish

Place the squash in a pot and add a small pinch of sea salt and the water. Cover and bring to a boil. Reduce the flame to medium-low and simmer several minutes, until the squash is soft. Remove the squash and purée in a hand food mill to a creamy consistency. Place back in the pot, season with sea salt, and continue to cook another 10 minutes or so. Place in serving bowls, garnish, and serve.

Variations. Substitute the following for squash: carrots, cauliflower, broccoli, or summer squash.

Seitan Vegetable Stew

---

2 cups cooked seitan
1 strip kombu, 3-4 inches long, soaked and cubed
1/2 cup onion, sliced in thick wedges
1 cup carrots, sliced in chunks
1/2 cup celery, sliced on a thick diagonal
1 cup Brussels sprouts, washed and sliced in half
1/4 cup burdock, sliced on a diagonal
1/4 cup leeks, sliced on a thick diagonal
4 cups water or tamari-seasoned cooking water from seitan
4 tablespoons kuzu, diluted in 4-5 tablespoons water
Tamari soy sauce
Sliced scallions for garnish

Layer ingredients in the following order: kombu, celery, onion, carrots, Brussels sprouts, leeks, burdock, and seitan. Add the water and bring to a boil. Cover and reduce the flame to medium-low. Simmer until the vegetables are soft. Season with a small amount of tamari soy sauce for a mild salt taste and simmer for several more minutes. Add the diluted kuzu, stirring constantly to prevent lumping. When thick, reduce the flame to low and simmer for 2-3 minutes. Place in individual serving bowls and garnish with sliced scallions.

Simple Vegetable Stew

By omitting the seitan in the previous recipe, you can prepare a simple vegetable stew. On occasion, vegetables may also be sautéed before cooking for a slightly different, richer flavor. Another variation is to substitute pan-fried or deep-fried tofu or tempeh for seitan to create variety.

Fish and Vegetable Soup
---

1 1/2 pounds white meat fish (scrod, cod,
    haddock, sole, etc.)
4-5 cups water
1/2 cup onion, sliced in thick wedges
1 cup carrots, sliced in chunks
1/4 cup celery, sliced on a thick diagonal
1/2 cup daikon, quartered and sliced in 1/4-
    inch pieces
2 tablespoons burdock, quartered and
    sliced
1 strip kombu, 1-2 inches long, soaked and
    diced
Sea salt, tamari soy sauce, or puréed bar-
    ley miso
Sliced scallions or parsley for garnish

Place the kombu in a pot and add the onion, celery, daikon, carrots, and burdock. Add the water and a small pinch of sea salt. Cover and bring to a boil. Reduce the flame to medium-low and simmer until the vegetables are soft and tender. Add the fish, cover, and reduce the flame to low. Simmer 4-5 minutes until the fish is done. Season with a small amount of sea salt, tamari soy sauce, or puréed barley miso for a mild salt taste. Simmer 5-10 minutes more if using sea salt, or 2-3 minutes if using tamari soy sauce or puréed miso. Garnish and serve hot.

You may occasionally add a small amount of grated ginger at

the end of cooking for a different flavor. Please feel free to use other ground or root vegetables instead of the ones listed.

VEGETABLES

Roughly one quarter to one third (25 to 30 percent) of each person's daily intake can include vegetables. Nature provides an incredible variety of local vegetables to choose from. Those recommended for regular use are listed in Table 5.2.

Vegetables can be served in soups or with grains, beans, or sea vegetables. They can also be used in making rice rolls (homemade sushi), served with noodles or pasta, cooked with fish, or served alone. The cooking methods used for vegetables include boiling, steaming, pressing, sautéeing (both with water and with oil), and pickling. A variety of natural seasonings, including miso, tamari soy sauce, sea salt, and brown rice or umeboshi vinegar, is recommended. To ensure adequate variety in the selection of vegetables, it is recommended that three to five vegetable side dishes be eaten daily.

The following methods are used often in cooking vegetables.

Steaming

Steaming produces a light, refreshing quality, and can be used daily or often to prepare vegetables. Steaming can be used for most vegetables, and there are two basic methods.

With a steamer basket. Steamer baskets are available in two styles. One is a stainless steel collapsable basket that fits inside a cooking pot. The other is a bamboo basket that fits on top of a cooking pot. To use these steamers, place about 1/2 inch of water in a pot. Set the stainless steel steamer down inside the pot or place the bamboo steamer on top of the pot. Next, slice your vegetables and place them in the steamer. Cover and bring the water to a boil. Steam until the vegetables are tender. When steaming greens, try to make sure the vegetables are tender but still bright green and slightly crisp. A few drops of tamari soy sauce can occasionally be sprinkled on the vegetables at the end of cooking for a different flavor.

Table 5.2.   Vegetables

For Regular Use	For Occasional Use	Avoid for Optimal Health and Vitality
Acorn Squash	Celery	Artichokes
Bok choy	Chives	Bamboo shoots
Broccoli	Coltsfoot	Beets
Brussels sprouts	Cucumber	Curly dock
Burdock	Endive	Eggplant
Butternut squash	Escarole	Fennel
Cabbage	Green beans	Ferns
Carrots	Green peas	Ginseng
Carrot tops	Iceberg lettuce	Green/Red pepper
Cauliflower	Jerusalem	New Zealand
Chinese cabbage	artichoke	spinach
Collard greens	Kohlrabi	Okra
Daikon	Lambsquarters	Plantain
Daikon greens	Mushrooms	Potato
Dandelion roots	Patty pan squash	Purslane
Dandelion leaves	Romaine lettuce	Shepherd's purse
Hokkaido	Salsify	Sorrel
pumpkin	Shiitake	Spinach
Hubbard squash	mushroom	Sweet potato
Jinenjo	Snap beans	Swiss chard
Kale	Snow peas	Taro (albi) potato
Leeks	Sprouts	Tomato
Lotus root	Summer squash	Yams
Mustard greens	Wax beans	Zucchini
Onion		
Parsley		
Parsnip		
Pumpkin		
Radish		
Red cabbage		
Rutabaga		
Scallions		
Turnip		
Turnip greens		
Watercress		

Without a steamer basket. To steam vegetables without a steamer, place about 1/4-1/2 inch of water in a pot and bring to a boil. Place the vegetables in the boiling water, cover, and steam for 2-5 minutes or until tender, depending on the type of vegetables used. Again, at the very end of cooking you may sprinkle a few drops of tamari soy sauce over the vegetables for a different flavor.

Steamed Greens

This particular dish may be eaten daily or often. To prepare, take greens such as turnip, daikon, carrot tops, kale, parsley, watercress, collards, cabbage, Chinese cabbage, or radish tops. Wash and slice them, and place them in a steamer or in a small amount of boiling water. Cover and steam several minutes until tender but still bright green.

If you are steaming several types of vegetables, it is best to do each separately to ensure even, proper cooking. They may be mixed after cooking. Also, the stems of green vegetables are often harder than the leafy portion and are best steamed separately or at least chopped very finely before steaming.

It is convenient to use a steamer basket for this method of cooking and to take about 2-3 minutes for steaming, depending upon the quantity and thickness of the vegetables used.

You may save the water from steaming for use as a soup stock or as a base for a vegetable sauce that can be thickened with kuzu and lightly seasoned with sea salt, tamari soy sauce, or puréed miso. Serve over the vegetables.

Boiling (Blanching) Vegetables

In Japanese, this style of cooking is called *ohitashi*. Wash the kale and leave either whole or slice. Place 2-3 inches of water in a pot and bring to a boil. Place the kale in the water, cover, and boil 1-2 minutes, until deep green but slightly crisp. Remove, drain, and place in a serving bowl.

The kale may be served plain or with a sauce such as kuzu, tamari-ginger, or sesame-umeboshi dressing. You may also garnish with roasted seeds or a little gomashio.

Other green vegetables can also be cooked this way. Boil for a very short time until the vegetables are tender, but still have a crisp texture and a deep, vibrant color. The cooking time depends upon the vegetable. For example, watercress takes only 35-40 seconds, while collard greens may take 1-2 minutes.

Boiled (Blanched) Salad

This dish can be served daily or often. Many kinds of boiled salad can be prepared simply by varying the combination of vegetables or the type of dressing served with the salad. Boiled salad can be served with or without dressing. The following recipe is an example of boiled salad.

> 1 cup Chinese cabbage, washed and sliced on a diagonal
> 1 cup watercress, washed and left whole
> 1/4 cup carrots, sliced in matchsticks
> 2 tablespoons celery, sliced on a thin diagonal
> Water

Place 2-3 inches of water in a pot and bring to a boil. Place the Chinese cabbage in the pot, cover, and boil for 1-2 minutes or until tender but still a little crisp. Remove, place in a strainer, and allow to drain and cool. Next, place the carrots in the boiling water, cover, and simmer for 1 minute or so. Remove, drain, and allow to cool. Next do the celery, then the watercress. After draining the watercress, you may slice it in 1-inch lengths. Place all the cooked vegetables in a serving bowl and mix. Serve plain or with a dressing.

Variations. The following combinations of vegetables can be used in Boiled Salad.

- Kale, carrots, cabbage, and onions
- Celery and carrots
- Watercress, Chinese cabbage, and sliced red radish
- Daikon, carrots, Chinese cabbage, and turnip greens
- Broccoli, carrots, onion, and cabbage

When making boiled salad, it is best to cook each vegetable separately in the same water. Cook the vegetables with the sweeter or more neutral tastes first, such as onions, daikon, or Chinese cabbage. Then do the stronger and bitter-tasting ones like celery, burdock, and watercress.

Salad Dressing Suggestions

- Purée 1 umeboshi plum or 1 teaspoon umeboshi paste with 1/2 cup of water in a suribachi. Chopped parsley, scallions, or roasted sesame seeds may also be blended in for variety.

- Dilute 1/2 teaspoon barley miso in 1/2 cup warm water and add about 1/2-1 teaspoon brown rice vinegar. Mix.

- Dilute 1 teaspoon tamari with 1/2 cup water and a small amount of chopped parsley. Mix.

- Lightly sprinkle a desired macrobiotic condiment on the salad.

Nishime

Nishime is another method of boiling and is sometimes referred to as "waterless cooking" because of the low volume of water used. Root or round-shaped vegetables are mostly used and are cut in large chunks or rounds. The vegetables are placed in a very small amount of water and cooked on a low flame for 35-40 minutes or so. A heavy stainless steel pot with a heavy cover is recommended for this type of cooking. Pan-fried, deep-fried, or fresh tofu and tempeh may be cooked with the vegetables, as may dried tofu, seitan, or fu.

This style of cooking produces a very sweet flavor and soft texture, and because of the slow, peaceful cooking process, imparts relaxing and calming energy.

Nishime

---

1 strip kombu, washed, soaked, and cut
    into 1-inch squares
1 cup daikon, sliced in 1-inch-thick rounds
1/2 cup carrots, sliced in chunks
1 cup buttercup or butternut squash or
    Hokkaido pumpkin, sliced in large
    chunks
1/4 cup burdock, sliced on a thick
    diagonal
1/4 cup fresh lotus root, sliced in 1/4-inch
    rounds
1/4 cup turnips, sliced in thick chunks
1 cup cabbage, sliced in 2-inch-thick
    chunks
Water
Pinch of sea salt
Tamari soy sauce

Place the kombu on the bottom of the pot and add about 1/2 inch of water. Layer the vegetables on top of the kombu in the following order: daikon, turnips, squash, carrots, lotus root, burdock, and cabbage. Add a pinch of sea salt, cover, and bring to a boil. Reduce the flame to low and simmer for 30-35 minutes or until the vegetables are soft and sweet. Add several drops of tamari soy sauce, cover, and simmer for another 5 minutes or so until almost all remaining liquid is gone. Mix the vegetables to evenly coat them with the sweet cooking liquid that remains. Place in a serving bowl.

Daikon, Kombu, and Daikon Greens

---

2 cups daikon, sliced in 1/2-inch-thick
    rounds
1 strip kombu, 2-3 inches long, soaked and
    cubed
1 cup daikon greens, sliced
Water
Tamari soy sauce

Place the kombu in a pot and set the daikon rounds on top. Add about 1/2-1 inch of water, cover the pot, and bring to a boil. Reduce the flame to medium-low and simmer for 20-30 minutes or so until the daikon and kombu are soft and tender. Season with a small amount of tamari soy sauce. Then place the greens on top of the daikon, cover, and simmer 2-3 minutes until the greens become tender but still bright green. Mix and serve.

Dried Daikon, Shiitake, and Kombu

---

1 cup dried daikon, rinsed, soaked in water
  10 minutes, and sliced
4 shiitake mushrooms, soaked 10 minutes,
  stems removed and sliced in thin slices
1 strip kombu, 4 inches long, soaked and
  sliced in thin matchsticks
Tamari soy sauce
Water

Place the kombu in a heavy skillet or pot and add the shiitake mushrooms and dried daikon. Include enough of the water from soaking the kombu, dried daikon, and shiitake to cover half or three-quarters of the daikon. Cover, bring to a boil, and reduce the flame to medium-low. Simmer for 35-40 minutes until soft and sweet. Add a small amount of tamari soy sauce for a mild taste, cover, and continue to cook several minutes until all the liquid is gone.

Sautéing

There are several ways to sauté vegetables. The following are used most often in macrobiotic cooking.

Oil Sautéing

For persons in generally good health, vegetables may be sautéed in high-quality vegetable oil 2-3 times per week on average. With this style of sautéing, a few drops of water can sometimes be added for extra moisture and to speed the cooking process. The vegetables may be finely sliced or cut in larger pieces. Leafy greens can be prepared in this way, as can root or ground vegetables.

Water Sautéing

This method is especially good for those who wish to limit their intake of oil. Place enough water in a skillet to just cover the bottom and heat up. Add the vegetables and sauté as you would if you were using oil. Season either with sea salt or several drops of tamari.

Water-Sautéed Vegetables

1/2 cup onion, sliced in thin half-moons
1/2 cup carrot, sliced in thin matchsticks
1/2 cup Chinese cabbage, sliced on a thin
    diagonal
1/4 cup celery, sliced on a thin diagonal
Tamari soy sauce
Water

Place enough water in a skillet to just cover the bottom, and heat up. Add the onion and sauté 1-2 minutes. Add the celery and sauté 1-2 minutes. Place the carrots in the skillet and sauté 2-3 minutes. Set the Chinese cabbage on top of the other vegetables. Add a few more drops of water, cover, and reduce the flame to medium-low. Simmer 3-4 minutes until tender but still crisp. Add a few drops of tamari, cover, and simmer another 1-2 minutes. Remove the cover and cook off any remaining liquid.

Kinpira

This style of cooking combines elements of sautéing and boiling and is similar to braising. It is used mostly for root vegetables. Vegetables are thinly sliced and cut in matchsticks, or in the case of burdock, shaved and then sautéed for several minutes in a small amount of sesame oil. (Those with restricted oil intakes may water sautée instead.) A small amount of water is then added to half-cover the vegetables or lightly cover the bottom of the skillet. The vegetables are then covered and cooked on a medium-low flame until tender. A small amount of tamari soy sauce can be added for a mild salt taste, and the vegetables are covered again and cooked for another several minutes. The cover is then removed and the remaining liquid is cooked away.

This style of cooking is also used for arame or hijiki sea vegetables.

Carrot and Burdock Kinpira

---

1 cup burdock, shaved
1 cup carrot, sliced in
  matchsticks
Water
Tamari soy sauce
Dark sesame oil (optional)

Place a small amount of dark sesame oil in a skillet and heat up. Add the burdock and sauté for 2-3 minutes. Set the carrots on top of the burdock. Do not mix. Add enough water to lightly cover the bottom of the skillet and bring to a boil. Cover and reduce the flame to medium-low. Cook several minutes until the vegetables are about 80 percent done. This may take 7-10 minutes. Add a few drops of tamari soy sauce, cover, and cook for several more minutes. Remove the cover and cook until all the remaining liquid evaporates.

Raw Vegetables

Persons in generally good health may enjoy raw salad several times per week, on average. Vegetables such as radish, celery, cabbage, carrot, lettuce, cucumber, and other recommended varieties may be used. The salad dressings presented in this section may be used together with others listed in macrobiotic cookbooks.

Pressed Vegetables

Pressed vegetables (often referred to as "pressed salad") are light and refreshing. They may be eaten daily, about 1/2 cup per serving. Pressed vegetables are combined with a salty pickling agent, such as sea salt or umeboshi vinegar, and are pressed for 2 hours or more. When done, the vegetables are lightly pickled instead of raw, and are easier to digest. Pressed salad can be prepared in the following ways.

With a pickle press. A pickle press is a specially made plastic jar. It comes in several sizes, with screw-on lids and a moveable plastic plate that fits inside for applying pressure. Pickle presses are available at most natural foods stores. To prepare pressed salad, slice the vegetables very thin and place in a bowl. Add a small amount of either sea salt, sea salt and brown rice vinegar, or umeboshi vinegar, and mix well. Put the chopped vegetables in the pickle press and place the cover on top. Screw the plate down to apply pressure. Let the vegetables sit for 2-4 hours before serving. If they are too salty, rinse them quickly under cold water and squeeze out any excess liquid.

With bowl and plate. If you do not have a pickle press, you can make one. Simply slice your vegetables as described above, place in a bowl with one of the above-mentioned pickling agents, and mix well. Take a plate or saucer that is a little smaller than the bowl and place it down inside so that it rests on top of the vegetables. Next, fill a large glass jar with water or take a heavy, clean rock and place it on top of the plate for pressure. Let sit for 2-4 hours. If too salty when done, simply rinse quickly under cold water and squeeze out any excess liquid.

Pressed Salad

---

2 cups lettuce, thinly sliced
1/4 cup celery, sliced on a thin diagonal
1/2 cup cucumber, sliced in thin rounds
1/4 cup onion, sliced in very thin rounds
1/4 cup red radish, sliced in very thin
    rounds
2-3 tablespoons umeboshi vinegar

Place all ingredients in a bowl and mix well. Place in a pickle press or bowl and apply pressure. Let sit for 2-4 hours. Remove and squeeze out excess liquid. If too salty, rinse quickly under cold water, then squeeze out the excess liquid.

Pickling

Refer to the section on pickles (page 175) for specific recipes or suggestions.

Other Methods

Baking and pressure cooking tend to make the energy in vegetables become more concentrated or drying. These methods are not recommended for regular use in preparing vegetables. A lighter and fresher quality of energy is preferred for regular use.

Pressure cooking is the most common method of cooking brown rice in macrobiotic households. It is a concentrated form of boiling that reduces the loss of minerals and other nutrients that would escape in steam during the boiling process. Pressure is a more contracting factor, squeezing moisture from foods and making them more concentrated.

BEANS AND BEAN PRODUCTS

Beans and bean products may be eaten daily or often so that they comprise about 5 to 10 percent of daily intake. See Table 5.3 for a list of beans and bean products that may be used in cooking.

Most beans require soaking for 6-8 hours before cooking to make them softer and more digestible. Exceptions to this are green lentils and split peas, which are soft in comparison with other beans, and cook more quickly. Beans may be soaked in cold, warm, or hot water. Soaking beans in cold water gives them a slightly firmer texture, but they may require more cooking time than beans soaked in hot water. Warm water makes the beans softer, more easy to digest, and quicker to cook. If you use hot water, beans only need to be soaked for 4-6 hours.

With the exception of azuki beans and black soybeans, the water from soaking beans can be discarded. The soaking water from azuki beans and black soybeans may be added during cooking.

It is best to cook beans with a small strip of the sea vegetable kombu. The minerals in the kombu soften the hard outer shell of the beans, making them more digestible. Kombu also enhances their flavor.

Table 5.3.   Beans and Bean Products

For Regular Use	For Occasional Use	Bean Products for Occasional Use
Azuki beans	Black-eyed peas	Dried tofu
Black soybeans	Black turtle beans	Fresh tofu
Chickpeas	Great northern	Natto
(Garbanzo beans)	beans	Tempeh
Lentils (green)	Kidney beans	
	Mung beans	
	Navy beans	
	Pinto beans	
	Soybeans	
	Split peas	
	Whole dried peas	

The most frequently recommended methods for cooking bean side dishes are the following.

Boiling. Place 1 cup dried, soaked beans in a pot, and add a 3- or 4-inch piece of kombu and 3 1/2-4 cups of cold water. Bring to a boil, cover, and reduce the flame to medium-low. Simmer until the beans are about 80 percent done. Season with 1/4 teaspoon sea salt per cup of uncooked beans, or the equivalent amount of tamari soy sauce or puréed miso. Cover the pot and simmer until the beans are soft. When done, remove the cover and boil off any excess until you have the desired consistency.

Shocking Method. Place a 3- or 4-inch strip of kombu in a pot and set 1 cup of soaked beans on top. Add 2 1/2 cups of water per cup of beans. Leave the pot uncovered and cook slowly on a low flame until the water comes to a boil. Place a lid that is smaller than the pot down inside the pot so that it rests on the beans. The lid will keep the beans from jumping around. As the beans cook, they will expand in size. Occasionally pour a small amount of water gently down the side of the pot as needed. Continue to cook until the beans are about 80 percent done. At this point, season, leave the cover off, and continue to cook until the beans are soft. Turn up the heat and cook off any excess liquid that remains.

Azuki Beans with Kombu and Squash

---

1 cup azuki beans, soaked 4-6 hours
1 cup cubed hard winter squash (use acorn,
    buttercup, or butternut squash, or
    Hokkaido pumpkin; carrots or parsnips
    may be substituted if squash is not
    available)
1 strip kombu, 1-2 inches long, soaked and
    diced
Water
Sea salt

Place the kombu on the bottom of a pot. Set the squash on top. Place the azuki beans on top of the squash. Add water to just cover the squash. Bring to a boil, cover, and reduce the flame to low. Simmer until about 80 percent done. Season with 1/4 teaspoon of sea salt per cup of beans, cover, and continue to cook another 15-20 minutes until soft and creamy.

Variations. The following combinations of vegetables may be used in Azuki Beans with Kombu and Squash.

- 1 cup azuki beans, 1/2 cup lotus seeds, kombu

- 1 cup azuki beans, 1/2 cup dried chestnuts, kombu

- 1 cup azuki beans, 1/4 cup soaked wheat berries, kombu

- 1 cup azuki beans, 1/4 cup dried apples, 1 tablespoon raisins, kombu (can be used as a sweet dessert)

Use either of the methods described on page 163 to prepare.

Soybeans and Kombu

---

1 cup soybeans, soaked 6-8 hours in 2 1/2
   cups water
1 strip kombu, 6 inches long, soaked and
   cubed
2 1/2 cups water
Tamari soy sauce

Drain off the soaking water and place the kombu and soybeans in a pressure cooker. Add fresh water and boil for 15 minutes, skimming off any skins that float to the surface. Cover the pressure cooker and bring up to pressure. Reduce the flame to medium-low and cook for approximately 50 minutes. Remove from the flame and allow the pressure to come down. Remove the cover, add a small amount of tamari soy sauce, and simmer uncovered for another 5-10 minutes. Remove, garnish, and serve.

Variations. The following combinations of vegetables may be used in Soybeans and Kombu.

* Soybeans, kombu, onion, and carrots
* Soybeans, kombu, carrots, lotus root, burdock, seitan, celery, shiitake mushrooms, and dried daikon (thicken at the end of cooking with a small amount of diluted kuzu).

Black Soybeans

Black soybeans are washed and soaked in a slightly different way from other beans because of their soft skins. To wash, first dampen a clean kitchen towel. Place the beans in the towel and cover completely. Roll the bean-filled towel back and forth several times to rub off dust and soil. Place the beans in a bowl, dampen the towel again, and repeat. This can be done 2-3 times until the beans are clean. After washing the beans, place them in a bowl. Add about 3 cups of water for each cup of beans, and 1/4 teaspoon of sea salt. Soak the beans 6-8 hours or overnight.

Place the beans in a pot with the salt-seasoned soaking water and bring to a boil. Do not cover the beans. Reduce the flame to medium-low and simmer until the beans are about 90 percent done, which may take about 2-3 hours. During cooking you may need to add water occasionally, but add only enough to just cover the beans each time. As the beans cook, a gray foam will rise to the surface. Skim off and discard. Repeat until the foam no longer appears. When the beans are almost done (tender), add several drops of tamari soy sauce. Do not mix with a spoon. You may, however, gently shake the pot up and down 2-3 times to mix the beans and coat them with bean juice, which will make the skins a very shiny black color. Continue cooking until no liquid remains. Total cooking time varies from 3-3 1/2 hours.

Chickpeas and Vegetables
---

1 cup chickpeas, soaked 6-8 hours or overnight
1 cup carrots, sliced in chunks
1 cup parsnips, sliced in chunks
1 strip kombu, 1-2 inches long, soaked and
   diced
Water
Sea salt or puréed barley miso

Place the kombu, parsnips, carrots, and chickpeas in a pot and add water to just cover. Prepare using either of the methods described on page 163. When 80 percent done, season with tamari soy sauce, sea salt, or puréed barley miso. If boiling, chickpeas may take 3-4 hours.

Green Lentils with Onion and Kombu
---

1 cup green lentils
1 cup onion, sliced in thick wedges
1 strip kombu, 2 inches long, soaked and
   diced
Sea salt
Water

Place the kombu in a pot and set the onion on top. Add the lentils. Add enough water to just cover the lentils. Bring to a boil, reduce the flame to medium-low, and cover. Simmer about 35 minutes or until tender. Occasionally during cooking you may need to add small amounts of water, as the beans absorb liquid and expand. Each time, add just enough water to cover the lentils. When the lentils are almost done, season them with approximately 1/4 teaspoon of sea salt per cup of beans. Cover and simmer another 10-15 minutes.

Variations. The following combinations of vegetables may be used in Green Lentils with Onion and Kombu.

- Lentils, onion, carrots, celery, kombu
- Lentils, onion, carrots, burdock, celery, kombu, and parsley

---
Dried Tofu with Kombu and Carrots

1/2 cup dried tofu, soaked and cubed or
    sliced in rectangles
1 cup carrots, sliced in thick matchsticks
1 strip kombu, 2-3 inches long, soaked and
    sliced in very thin matchsticks
Water
Tamari soy sauce

To soak the dried tofu, place in warm water for about 10 minutes. Squeeze out the water. Rinse under cold water and squeeze again. Discard the soaking water and slice.

Place the kombu in a pot. Add the dried tofu and carrots. Add enough water to just cover the dried tofu and bring to a boil. Reduce the flame to medium-low, cover, and simmer about 25-30 minutes or until the kombu is soft. Add several drops of tamari soy sauce, cover, and continue to cook for 3-5 minutes. Remove the cover and simmer until excess liquid is gone.

Scrambled Tofu
---

1 one-pound cake fresh tofu, drained
1/2 cup diced onion
1/2 cup carrots, sliced in
    matchsticks
1/4 cup burdock, sliced in
    matchsticks
1/4 cup celery, sliced on a thin
    diagonal
Dark sesame oil
Tamari soy sauce
Chopped scallion garnish

Brush a small amount of dark sesame oil in the bottom of a skillet and heat up. Add the onions and sauté 1-2 minutes. Next add the celery and sauté 1-2 minutes. Set the carrots and burdock on top of the celery and onions. Crumble the tofu and spread it on top of the vegetables. Cover and bring to a boil.

Reduce the flame to medium-low and simmer until the tofu is soft and fluffy and the vegetables are tender. Add a small amount of chopped scallions and several drops of tamari. Cover and simmer another 2-3 minutes.

Tempeh with Sauerkraut and Cabbage

---

1 cup cubed tempeh
1 cup shredded green
    cabbage
1/4 cup chopped sauerkraut
Small amount of sauerkraut
    juice
Tamari soy sauce

Heat a skillet and add the tempeh cubes. Place a drop of tamari on each cube and brown slightly. Add the sauerkraut and cabbage. Add enough sauerkraut juice or plain water to half-cover the tempeh. Bring to a boil, cover, and reduce the flame to low. Simmer about 20-25 minutes. Remove the cover and cook off any remaining liquid.

SEA VEGETABLES

Sea vegetables may be used daily in cooking. Side dishes can be made with arame or hijiki and included several times per week. Wakame and kombu can be used daily in miso and other soups, in vegetable and bean dishes, or as condiments. Toasted nori is also recommended for daily or regular use, while agar-agar can be used from time to time in making a natural jelled dessert known as kanten. Table 5.4 lists the sea vegetables used in macrobiotic cooking.

Table 5.4. Sea Vegetables

For Regular Use (almost daily)	For Occasional or Optional Use
Arame	Agar agar
Hijiki	Dulse
Kombu	Irish moss
Wakame	Mekabu
Toasted nori	Sea palm
	Other traditionally used sea vegetables

Arame with Carrots and Onions

---

1 ounce dried arame, rinsed, drained, and
   allowed to sit 3-5 minutes
1/2 cup onion, sliced in half-moons
1/2 cup carrots, sliced in matchsticks
Dark sesame oil
Water
Tamari soy sauce

Lightly brush dark sesame oil in a skillet and heat up. Place the onion in the skillet and sauté 1-2 minutes. Place the sliced carrots on top of the onion. Slice the arame and set on top of the carrots. Do not mix. Add enough water to just cover the vegetables but not the arame, then add a very small amount of tamari. Bring to a boil, reduce the flame to medium-low, and cover. Simmer for about 35-40 minutes, then lightly season with a few drops of tamari for a mild salt taste. Cover and cook another 5-7 minutes. Remove the cover and continue to cook until almost all liquid is gone. Mix and cook off remaining liquid. Garnish and serve.

Hijiki with Onions and Lotus Root

Depending on the texture or hardness of the hijiki, the cooking time may vary. Softer varieties of hijiki may only need to be cooked 30-40 minutes until soft, while harder varieties may require as much as 1 hour cooking time. Please adjust the cooking time depending on the variety of hijiki that is available to you.

> 1 ounce hijiki, washed, soaked 3-5
>   minutes, and sliced
> 1/2 cup onion, sliced in thin half-moons
> 1/2 cup fresh lotus root, washed, halved,
>   and thinly sliced
> Dark sesame oil
> Water
> Tamari soy sauce

Lightly brush dark sesame oil in a skillet and heat. Add the onion and sauté 1-2 minutes. Add the lotus root and sauté 1-2 minutes. Place the hijiki on top of the vegetables. Add enough water to cover the vegetables but not the hijiki. Bring to a boil, cover, and reduce the flame to medium-low. Simmer for 30-45 minutes depending on the texture or hardness of the hijiki. Season with a few drops of tamari for a mild salt taste, cover, and continue to cook another 10-15 minutes. Remove the cover, mix, and simmer until all remaining liquid is gone. Garnish and serve.

Boiled Kombu with Carrots and Burdock

> 2 strips kombu, 6 inches long, soaked and
>   cubed
> 1 cup burdock, sliced on thick diagonals
> 1 1/2 cups carrots, sliced in chunks
> Water
> Tamari soy sauce

Place the kombu in the bottom of a pot. Add the burdock and carrots. Add enough water to half-cover the vegetables. Bring to a boil, cover, and reduce the flame to medium-low. Simmer for 30-35 minutes or until the kombu and vegetables are soft and tender. Season with a few drops of tamari, cover, and simmer another 5-10 minutes. Remove the cover and cook off all remaining liquid. Mix and serve.

Wakame, Onion, and Carrots

---

1 ounce dried wakame, washed, soaked,
  and sliced
1/2 cup onion, sliced in thick wedges
1/2 cup carrots, sliced in chunks
Water
Tamari soy sauce

Place the onion, carrots, and wakame in a pot. Add enough water to half-cover the vegetables. Bring to a boil, cover, and reduce the flame to medium-low. Simmer 25-30 minutes or until the vegetables are soft. Add a few drops of tamari soy sauce for a mild salt taste. Cover and simmer another 10-15 minutes.

Toasted Nori

Nori, a light, thin sea vegetable that usually comes in dried sheets, does not require washing or soaking. However, to increase its digestibility it can be dry roasted. Take a sheet of nori from the package and hold it so that the smooth, shiny side faces upward. Turn the flame on your stove to medium and hold the nori about six inches above it. Slowly rotate or move the nori above the flame until it changes from purplish brown to green. You may cut it into strips or squares for use as a garnish on soups, stews, noodles, or grains, or simply break off small pieces and eat as a snack. Toasted nori can also be used in making rice balls, triangles, and sushi by wrapping cooked rice and other ingredients inside it. Please see the section on grains for a recipe for rice triangles.

CONDIMENTS

A variety of condiments may be used, some daily and others occasionally. Small amounts may be used on grains, soups, vegetables, beans, and other dishes. Condiments allow everyone to freely adjust the taste and nutritional value of foods and stimulate and contribute to better appetite and digestion. The most frequently used varieties include the following.

Main Condiments

- Gomashio (a half-crushed mixture of roasted sesame seeds and roasted sea salt)
- Sea vegetable powder
- Sea vegetable powder with roasted sesame seeds
- Tekka (selected root vegetables sautéed with dark sesame oil and seasoned with soybean or hatcho miso)
- Umeboshi plum (pickled plums)

Other Condiments

- Cooked miso with scallions or onions
- Nori condiment (nori cooked with tamari soy sauce)
- Roasted sesame seeds
- Shiso leaf powder
- Shio kombu (kombu cooked with tamari soy sauce)
- Green nori flakes
- Brown rice vinegar (used mostly as a seasoning)
- Umeboshi plum and raw scallions or onions
- Umeboshi vinegar (used mostly as a seasoning)
- Other traditionally used condiments (not highly stimulating ones)

Gomashio (Sesame Salt)

---

1 cup black or tan sesame seeds, washed
  and drained
1 tablespoon sea salt

Place the sea salt in a hot skillet and dry roast several minutes over a medium flame until it becomes shiny. Remove and grind to a fine powder in a suribachi. Next, place the damp sesame seeds in a heated skillet and dry roast over a medium-low flame, stirring constantly with a wooden rice paddle. Shake the skillet back and forth occasionally to evenly roast. When the seeds give off a nutty fragrance and begin popping, take a seed and crush it between your thumb and ring finger. If it crushes easily, the seeds are done. If not, roast them a little longer. When the seeds are done, place them in the suribachi and slowly grind together with the sea salt. Continue grinding until the seeds are about half crushed. Allow to cool and store in a tightly sealed glass container. Use moderately on grains, noodles, or vegetable dishes.

Sea Vegetable Powders

Take several pieces of kombu, wakame, or dulse and place them, unwashed, on a baking sheet. Roast in a 350° F oven for approximately 15-20 minutes or until crispy and dark but not burnt, or place in a dry skillet and roast until crispy and dark. Remove and break the roasted sea vegetable into small pieces over a suribachi. Crush into a fine powder. Allow to cool and store in a tightly sealed glass container. Sprinkle lightly on grains, noodles, or vegetable dishes.

Sea Vegetable and Roasted Sesame Seed Powders

Roast one of the sea vegetables as explained in the recipe for Sea Vegetable Powders. After roasting, grind into a fine powder in a suribachi. Dry roast washed and drained tan sesame seeds as you would if making gomashio. When done, place the roasted seeds in the suribachi and grind with the sea vegetable powder until the seeds are about half crushed. Allow to cool and store in a tightly sealed glass container. Use as you would gomashio or roasted sea vegetable powders. The average proportion of seeds to powdered sea vegetable can be about 40 to 60 percent.

Tekka

Tekka has been used in traditional cooking to strengthen vitality and increase energy in the intestines and lower body. It is a very strong condiment and should be used in moderation. Tekka is made from minced burdock, lotus root, carrot, hatcho miso, and dark sesame oil. Toward the end of cooking, it is seasoned with ginger juice. It is cooked over a low flame in a cast iron skillet until the ingredients turn completely black. Tekka can be purchased prepackaged in natural foods stores. Use moderately on grains, noodles, or vegetable dishes.

Nori Condiment

---

5 sheets nori, unroasted
Water
Tamari soy sauce

Tear the nori into small squares and place in a saucepan. Add water to just cover the nori. Bring to a boil, cover, and reduce the flame to low. Simmer until the nori becomes a smooth, thick paste. Season with several drops of tamari soy sauce for a mild salt taste and continue to cook until all the liquid is gone. Allow to cool and store in the refrigerator in a tightly sealed glass container. Eat with grains, noodles, or vegetable dishes. A small amount of freshly grated ginger may be added at the end of cooking for a special flavor.

Table 5.5. Pickles

For Regular Use	Avoid for Optimal Health
Amazake pickles	Dill pickles
Brine pickles	Garlic pickles
Miso bean pickles	Herb pickles
Miso pickles	Spiced pickles
Pressed pickles	Vinegar pickles (commercial
Rice bran pickles	apple cider vinegar or wine
Sauerkraut	vinegar pickles)
Takuan pickles	
Tamari soy sauce pickles	

PICKLES

A small amount of natural vegetable pickles can be eaten daily or often as a supplement to main dishes. They stimulate appetite and help digestion. Some varieties, such as pickled daikon or takuan, can be bought prepackaged in natural foods stores. Others, such as quick pickles, can be prepared at home. Table 5.5 lists those pickles that can be eaten regularly, and those that should be avoided.

Umeboshi-Vegetable Pickles

Place 7-8 umeboshi plums in a glass jar and add 2 quarts of water. Shake well and allow to sit several hours until the water becomes pink. Place a variety of thinly sliced vegetables (such as red radish, daikon, carrot, onion, cauliflower florets, broccoli florets, red onion, and cabbage) in the water. Cover the jar with clean cotton cheesecloth and store in a cool place for 3-5 days. When done, remove, or, if too salty, rinse quickly under cold water, and serve.

Quick Tamari Soy Sauce Vegetable Pickles

Slice a variety of root or ground vegetables into thin slices and place in a glass jar. Cover with a mixture of 1/2 water and 1/2 tamari soy sauce. Shake and cover the jar with clean cotton cheesecloth. Allow to sit in a cool place for 2-3 hours. Remove and serve, or, if too salty, rinse quickly and serve.

Three-Day Tamari Soy Sauce/Vegetable Pickles

Prepare as in previous recipe, but allow the vegetables to pickle in the tamari-water solution for 3-5 days. Remove, rinse, and serve.

Brine Pickles

Boil 3-4 cups of water together with 1 teaspoon of sea salt until the salt is completely dissolved. Allow to cool completely. Place a 3-inch piece of kombu in a jar and pour the cool salt brine over it. Place thin slices of root or ground vegetables such as carrots, daikon, radishes, onions, broccoli, cauliflower, and cucumber in the water. Cover the jar with clean cotton cheesecloth and let it sit in a slightly cool and dark place for 3 days (*not* the refrigerator). After 3 days, these pickles can be stored in the refrigerator.

Other Pickles

A variety of prepackaged pickles can be purchased at most natural foods stores, including daikon-rice bran pickles, takuan pickles, ginger pickles, and sauerkraut. If the pickles taste too salty, simply rinse or soak them for 1/2 hour before eating.

SUPPLEMENTARY FOODS

A variety of supplementary foods can be enjoyed occasionally. Some items can be eaten several times per week, and others, such as seasonings and beverages, are used daily but in smaller amounts than the foods listed above. Supplementary foods include the following.

White Meat Fish

For variety, enjoyment, and nourishment, fish and seafood may be enjoyed on occasion by those in ordinary good health. The frequency of eating fish and seafood varies according to climate, age, sex, and personal needs and can range from once in a while to more regularly. The standard is about once or twice per week in a temperate climate. See Table 5.6 for a list of white meat fish varieties.

Broiled or Grilled White Meat Fish

To broil or grill fish, marinate in a mixture of equal parts water and tamari soy sauce and a few drops of fresh ginger juice for 1 hour, or simply sprinkle with freshly squeezed lemon juice and a few drops of tamari soy sauce. Broil or grill until tender and flaky. Remove and serve with a garnish and grated daikon.

Table 5.6. White Meat Fish

Ocean Varieties	Fresh Water Varieties	Dried Fish
Cod	Bass	Bonito flakes (dried
Flounder	Carp	bonita, freshly
Haddock	Catfish	shredded)
Halibut	Pike	Chirimen Iriko
Herring	Trout	(very small dried
Ocean trout	Whitefish	fish)
Perch	Other varieties of	Dried white meat
Scrod	white meat fresh	fish
Shad	water fish	
Smelt		
Sole		
Other varieties of		
white meat ocean		
fish		

Note: Shellfish such as lobster, crabmeat, and shrimp are best limited or avoided for optimal health as they are high in cholesterol.

Steamed or Boiled White Meat Fish

Marinate or place plain fish in a steamer basket or saucepan. Steam or boil until tender and flaky. Remove and serve with a garnish and grated daikon.

Baked White Meat Fish

Marinate and bake as is, or stuff the fish fillets with thinly sliced vegetables, cover, and bake at 450-475°F for 20 minutes or until soft and tender. Serve with a garnish and grated daikon.

Variation. Bake with a thin layer of puréed miso covering the fish.

Fruit and Dessert

In general, fruit can be enjoyed on occasion by those in good health. Frequency of consumption varies according to climate, season, age, level of activity, and personal need and health considerations. The average is about two to four times per week.

Among fruits, locally grown or temperate climate varieties are preferred, especially for persons living in these regions. As much as possible, it is best to avoid consumption of tropical fruit. The varieties of fruit that can be eaten in a temperate climate are presented in Table 5.7 according to season of availability or optimal season for use.

Stewed Fruit with Kuzu
---

2 cups apple juice or water (or half and half)
1 cup sliced apples or pears
1 tablespoon raisins
Pinch of sea salt
3 heaping teaspoons kuzu

Table 5.7. Fruit

Spring	Summer	Autumn	Winter
Cherries	Apricots	Apples	Dried fruit
Dried fruit	Blueberries	Dried fruit	Pears
Plums	Cantaloupes	Grapes	Raisins
Strawberries	Cherries	Pears	
	Dried fruit	Raisins	
	Grapes		
	Peaches		
	Raisins		
	Raspberries		
	Strawberries		
	Tangerines		
	Watermelon		

Dried Fruit (Unsulphured) for Use in All Seasons	Avoid in a Temperate Climate
Apples	Bananas
Apricots	Dates
Cherries	Figs
Peaches	Pineapples
Pears	Other tropical fruits
Plums	
Prunes	
Raisins	

Place the raisins, apple juice or water, and pinch of sea salt in a pot and bring to a boil. Reduce the flame to medium-low, cover, and simmer until the apples are soft. Turn the flame down low. Dilute the kuzu in a small amount of water and pour it into the apple mixture, stirring constantly to prevent lumping. When thick, simmer 1 minute. Remove and serve.

Amazake Pudding

---

1 pint amazake
1 cup apples or pears
3 teaspoons diluted
    kuzu

Place the apples and amazake in a saucepan and bring to a boil. Reduce the flame to medium-low and simmer until the fruit is soft. Reduce the flame to low and add the diluted kuzu, stirring constantly to prevent lumping. Simmer 1 minute or so until thick. Remove and serve.

Baked Apples

Wash the apples, core, and place in a baking dish with a little water. Cover and bake at 350–375°F for about 30 minutes or until soft. Remove and serve.

Applesauce

Wash, peel if waxed, core, and slice the apples. Place in a pot with a pinch of sea salt. Add enough water to just lightly cover the bottom of the pot. Cover and bring to a boil. Reduce the flame to medium-low and simmer until the apples are soft. Purée in a hand food mill and serve.

Dried Chestnuts and Dried Apples

---

1 cup dried chestnuts
1/2 cup dried apples, soaked and sliced
2 1/2 cups water
Pinch of sea salt

Wash the chestnuts and dry-roast in a skillet over a low flame for several minutes. Remove and place in a pressure cooker. Add the water and allow the chestnuts to soak for about 10 minutes. Add the dried apples and pinch of sea salt. Place the cover on the pressure cooker and bring up to pressure. Reduce the flame to medium-low and simmer for about 40 minutes. Remove the cooker and allow the pressure to come down. Take the cover off and serve.

Azuki Beans, Chestnuts, and Raisins

1/2 cup azuki beans, soaked 6-8 hours
1/2 cup dried chestnuts, dry-roasted and
    soaked 10 minutes
2 tablespoons raisins
2 1/2 cups water
1 strip kombu, 2-3 inches long, soaked and
    diced
1/4 teaspoon sea salt

Place the kombu, azuki beans, chestnuts, raisins, and water in a pot. Cover and bring to a boil. Reduce the flame to medium-low and simmer for about 2-2 1/2 hours. As the beans are cooking, you may need to add a small amount of water from time to time. When the beans are just tender, season them with sea salt and simmer for another 15 minutes or until soft.

Kanten

4 cups water
2 cups dried apples, soaked and sliced
Agar-agar flakes (follow package instruc-
    tions for above amount of liquid)
Pinch of sea salt

Place the water, sea salt, dried apples, and kanten (agar-agar) flakes in a pot. Bring to a boil. Reduce the flame to low, cover, and simmer until the apples are soft. Remove and pour the apples and liquid into a dish. Refrigerate or place in a cool place until jelled. Kanten is usually ready to serve in 45-60 minutes. Slice or spoon into serving dishes.

NUTS

Nuts can be eaten from time to time as snacks and garnishes. It is best to keep their consumption occasional and to eat them in small amounts. Nuts that are roasted and lightly salted with natural sea salt or a small amount of tamari soy sauce are preferred. Among the many types of nuts, nontropical varieties that are lower in fat are recommended. Several varieties of nuts for use are listed in Table 5.8.

Roasted Nuts

Nuts can be roasted in two basic ways:

In the oven. Place the nuts on a baking sheet and bake in a 350°F oven until slightly brown. When they are almost done, add a few drops of tamari soy sauce and mix to evenly coat. Bake another 2-3 minutes.

In a skillet. Place a skillet on the stove and heat up. Add the nuts and reduce the flame to low. Stir constantly to evenly roast and prevent burning. Roast until light golden brown, sprinkle a few drops of tamari soy sauce on them, and roast for another minute or two. Remove and serve.

Variation. Dry roasted sea salt that has been ground to a fine powder in a suribachi may also be lightly sprinkled on roasted nuts instead of tamari soy sauce.

SEEDS

A variety of seeds may be eaten from time to time as snacks. They can be lightly roasted with or without salt. Varieties of seeds include the following.

- Pumpkin seeds
- Sesame seeds
- Sunflower seeds
- Other traditionally consumed seeds

Table 5.8. Nuts

For Occasional Use	Nuts to Avoid for Optimal Health (Tropical Varieties)
Almonds	Brazil nuts
Peanuts	Cashews
Pecans	Hazel nuts
Walnuts	Macadamia nuts
	Pistachio nuts

Roasted Pumpkin or Squash Seeds

Rinse the seeds under cold water and drain. Heat a skillet and place the damp seeds in it. Dry roast, stirring constantly until the seeds become golden brown and begin to puff up slightly and pop. Plain roasted unseasoned pumpkin or squash seeds are preferred, although on occasion you may season mildly with a few drops of tamari soy sauce, mix, and roast for another several seconds until the tamari soy sauce on the seeds becomes dry. Remove and place in a serving bowl.

SNACKS

A variety of natural, high-quality snacks can be eaten from time to time. They can be made from grains, beans, nuts or seeds, sea vegetables, and temperate climate fruits. The following foods can be used as snacks.

- Leftovers

- Noodles

- Popcorn (homemade and unbuttered)

- Puffed whole cereal grains

- Rice balls

- Rice cakes

- Seeds

- Homemade sushi (without sugar, seasoning, or MSG)

- Mochi (pounded, steamed sweet brown rice)

- Steamed sourdough bread

Steamed Sourdough Bread

Slice several pieces of whole wheat sourdough or any other unyeasted whole grain bread. You can use fresh or stale bread. Place about 1/2 inch of water in a pot. Insert a steamer basket and place the sliced bread in the steamer. Cover and bring the water to a boil. Reduce the flame to medium and steam 4-5 minutes or until the bread is soft and warm. Remove and serve as is, with naturally processed and salted sesame butter, miso-tahini spread, or other appropriate spreads.

Miso-Tahini Spread

2-3 tablespoons organic sesame tahini
Barley miso
1-2 tablespoons chopped scallions
Water

Place the tahini in a small saucepan. Add a small amount of barley miso (mugi miso) for a mild salt taste, together with the chopped scallions. Add several drops of water and mix well. Place on a medium flame and simmer 2-3 minutes until the scallions are cooked, mixing constantly to evenly cook to prevent burning. Remove and serve on steamed bread, rice cakes, or other appropriate snacks.

Variations. Substitute organic sesame butter for tahini, or add chopped onions or parsley instead of scallions.

SWEETS

The naturally sweet flavor of cooked vegetables is preferred for optimal health. One or several of the vegetables listed below can be included in dishes on a daily basis.

- Cabbage

- Carrots

- Daikon

- Onions

- Parsnips

- Pumpkin

- Squash

In addition, a small amount of concentrated sweeteners made from whole cereal grains may be included when craved. Dried chestnuts, which also impart a sweet flavor, may also be included on occasion, as may hot apple juice or cider. Additional sweeteners include the following.

- Amazake (fermented sweet rice drink)

- Barley malt

- Brown rice syrup

- Chestnuts (cooked)

- Hot apple cider (with a pinch of sea salt)

- Hot apple juice (with a pinch of sea salt)

- Mirin (fermented sweet brown rice liquid)

Amazake

Amazake can be used in making desserts and puddings or may simply be heated in a saucepan and used as an occasional beverage.

Barley Malt or Brown Rice Syrup

These sweeteners may be used occasionally in making desserts, added in small amounts to soft cooked breakfast cereals for a sweeter flavor, or added to bancha tea for an additional sweet flavor.

SEASONINGS

A variety of naturally processed seasonings are fine for regular use. Unrefined sea salt is used regularly in cooking whole grains, beans, and many vegetables. Tamari soy sauce, miso, and umeboshi plums that have been salted and pickled are also used frequently, but in general the use of seasonings is best kept moderate. Rather than using them to add a salty flavor to your dishes, it is better to use them to bring forth the natural light sweetness of the whole grains, vegetables, beans, and sea vegetables and other ingredients you are cooking with. The use of salt is a highly individual matter and is based on factors such as age, sex, activity, and climate.

Table 5.9 lists seasonings that are most commonly used in macrobiotic cooking.

BEVERAGES

A variety of natural beverages can be included for daily, regular, or occasional consumption. The frequency and amount of

Table 5.9.   Seasonings

For Regular Use	For Occasional Use	Avoid for Optimal Health and Vitality
Miso, especially barley (mugi) and soybean (hatcho)	Ginger	All commercial seasonings
	Horseradish	
	Mirin	All irradiated spices and herbs
Tamari soy sauce	Rice vinegar	
Unrefined white sea salt	Sesame oil (dark)	All stimulating and aromatic spices and herbs
	Umeboshi vinegar	
	Umeboshi plum or paste	

beverage intake vary according to the individual's personal condition and needs as well as the climate, season, and other environmental factors. Generally, it is advisable to drink comfortably and when thirsty and to avoid icy cold drinks. Table 5.10 lists beverages that are most often used in the practice of microbiotics.

Bancha Twig Tea (Kukicha)

Place 1 tablespoon of bancha twigs in 1 quart of water and bring to a boil. Reduce the flame to low. Simmer 1-3 minutes for a mild-tasting tea or up to 15 minutes for a stronger tea. Drink while hot.

Bancha Stem Tea

This tea is made entirely of twigs and contains no leaves. It is prepared in the same manner as Kukicha but requires a slightly longer cooking time.

Roasted Grain Tea

Dry roast about 1/2 cup of washed barley or brown rice in a skillet until golden yellow, stirring constantly to prevent burning. Place the roasted grain in a quart of water and bring to a boil. Reduce the flame to low and simmer for about 15-20 minutes. Drink while hot.

Roasted Barley Tea

You may purchase prepackaged, unhulled, roasted barley tea in most natural foods stores. Place 1 tablespoon of roasted barley in a quart of water and bring to a boil. Reduce the flame to low and simmer 1-2 minutes for a mild tea or up to 10 minutes for a stronger-flavored beverage. Drink while hot, or drink at room temperature in hotter weather.

Table 5.10.   Beverages

For Regular Use	For Occasional Use	Infrequent Use	Avoid for Optimal Health and Vitality
Bancha stem tea	Dandelion tea	Beer (natural quality)	Aromatic herbal teas
Bancha twig tea (Kukicha)	Freshly squeezed carrot juice (if desired, about 2 cups per week)	Green leaf tea	Artificial, chemically treated beverages
High-quality natural well water	Grain coffee (100 percent roasted cereal grains)	Green magma	Chemically colored tea
Natural spring water (suitable for daily use)	Kombu tea	Northern climate fruit juice	Coffee
Roasted barley tea	Mu tea	Sake (natural quality)	Cold or iced drinks
Roasted brown rice tea	Sweet vegetable broth	Vegetable juice	Distilled water
	Umeboshi tea	Wine (natural quality)	Hard liquor
			Mineral water and all bubbling waters
			Stimulant beverages
			Sugared drinks
			Tap water
			Tropical fruit juices

Afterword

Ultimately, women and men share the same origin in nature. They represent yin and yang, or the two hands of God. When they make love, they unite these opposite energies. By seeking each other, men and women are seeking oneness or harmony with the infinite universe.

The game of love is the game of life. Everyone and everything is playing it. Love or attraction takes place between plants, animals, atoms, and molecules. In a field of wheat, one stalk will be charged with heaven's energy, the next with earth's energy, and so on in an alternating pattern. The same harmony occurs between blades of grass and trees in a forest. Love or harmony exists everywhere and in all things. Nothing can exist outside of it.

As we have seen, how we eat and live has a great deal to do with love and sexual happiness. Food is the primary means by which we create health, or the vibrant flow of heaven and earth's forces through the body. It is also a means to create emotional and spiritual harmony. The term *Wa* is used in Japanese to describe this peaceful state. The character for Wa is made up of symbols that represent cereal grain and mouth. It means that when people eat whole grains and vegetables as their main foods, love and harmony prevail in their relationships with one another and with the universe.

Love is intangible and spiritual. It extends far beyond the world of the senses. That is why love can't be weighed, measured, or quantified. Love transcends these considerations and is unique to every individual.

Love comes naturally when we live in harmony with nature. On the other hand, the physical disorders, emotional distresses, and negative thoughts that result from living against nature disrupt the flow of energy in the body. Disharmony in body and mind are the reason why we so often lose sight of the love that exists throughout the universe and why we have trouble loving other people or ourselves.

Many things happen during the course of a lifetime. Couples experience joy and sadness, success and failure, health and sickness, togetherness and separation, birth and death. Life is constantly changing, and we must continually adapt to new circumstances. Love is essential if we are to pass through life's experiences and learn from them.

Sharing a dream is also important for a relationship. It isn't necessary for the dream to be totally clear or complete. A general sense of purpose or vision of the future are enough in the beginning. Dreams, such as making the world healthy and peaceful, creating a happy family, or simply sharing life with the person you love, give meaning and purpose to our daily existence.

Men and women rely on each other for support and encouragement of their dreams and ambitions. Ideally, life partners share the same dream and act together to realize it. As their dream unfolds throughout life, their love for each other can grow to include the boundless spiritual dimensions of their existence.

Clear and open communication is also important. Simple things like eating together, complimenting one another, and showing affection help keep the channels of communication open and active. One of the reasons why couples have so many problems communicating today is because they eat apart so often. This causes separation and makes communication and understanding more difficult.

Eating healthful home-cooked meals together creates a unity that makes it easier to talk freely and openly with each other about what you are doing, your likes and dislikes, and your dreams and aspirations. As time goes by, a man and woman can become like one mind and communicate without words. Ten or twenty years is not long enough for two people to really know each other. To understand the game of yin and yang and solve the eternal mystery of love takes a lifetime.

For Further Study

The recipes presented in Chapter 5 represent only a small sampling of the thousands of dishes used in macrobiotic cooking. For additional recipes and guidance on such preliminary steps as washing, storing, and cutting foods, and on meal planning, the following cookbooks are especially recommended.

Esko, Wendy. *Aveline Kushi's Introducing Macrobiotic Cooking.* Tokyo: Japan Publications, 1987.

Esko, Wendy and Edward. *Macrobiotic Cooking for Everyone.* Tokyo: Japan Publications, 1979.

Kushi, Aveline with Alex Jack. *Aveline Kushi's Complete Guide to Macrobiotic Cooking.* New York: Warner Books, 1985.

Kushi, Aveline and Wendy Esko. *The Changing Seasons Macrobiotic Cookbook.* Garden City Park, NY: Avery Publishing Group, 1985.

Kushi, Aveline. *How to Cook with Miso.* Tokyo: Japan Publications, 1979.

Kushi, Aveline. *The Macrobiotic Cancer Prevention Cookbook.* Garden City Park, NY: Avery Publishing Group, 1988.

Kushi, Aveline. *The Macrobiotic Food and Cooking Series.* Tokyo: Japan Publications (Four Volumes, 1985-1988).

Kushi, Aveline and Wendy Esko. *The Quick and Natural Macrobiotic Cookbook.* Chicago: Contemporary Books, 1989.

Kushi, Aveline and Wendy Esko. *Aveline Kushi's Wonderful World of Salads.* Tokyo: Japan Publications, 1989.

Index

Achilles tendon, 68, 86
Acorn squash. *See* Squash, acorn.
Acquired Immune Deficiency Syndrome.
    See AIDS.
Acupuncture, 5, 51
Agar-Agar, 45, 168, 181
AIDS, 79, 109
Alcohol, 47, 82, 91, 103, 116
Amazake, 88, 121, 179, 180, 185
Amazake pickles, 175
Amazake Pudding, 179-180
Amino acid, 43
Anemia, 85
Anger. *See* Emotions, negative.
Animal foods. *See* Foods, animals.
Anti-insulin. *See* Glucagon.
Anxiety, 32, 44, 83
Applesauce, 180
Arame, 45, 121, 159, 168, 169
Arame with Carrots and Onions, 169
Arthritis, 42
Asparagus, 42
Atherosclerosis, 35
Avocado, 42, 92
Azuki beans, 43, 44, 121, 132-133,143-
    144, 162, 163, 164, 181
Azuki Beans, Chestnuts, and Raisins, 181
Azuki Bean Soup, 143-144
*Azuki Beans with Kombu and
    Squash,* 163-164

Baked Apples, 180
Baked White Meat Fish, 178
Baking. *See* Food preparation methods.
Bancha Stem Tea, 187
Bancha tea, 48, 93-94, 118, 187
Bancha Twig Tea (Kukicha), 187

Barley, 37, 39, 47, 106, 120,135-136, 187
Barley malt, 185, 186
Barley miso. *See* Miso, barley.
Basic Pressure-Cooked Brown Rice, 129
Basic Vegetable-Miso Soup, 141-142
Bean/bean products, 39, 43-45, 46, 52, 78,
    89, 106, 125, 126, 132, 162-168. *See
    also* Soybeans.
Beets, 42
Beverages, 48, 91, 115, 116, 122, 126,
    186-188
Birth control. *See* Sexual problems and
    modern lifestyle, birth control.
Birth control pill, 79-80, 122
Black Bean Rice, 133
Black soybeans, 43, 121, 132, 133, 162,
    165
Black Soybeans, 165
Blanching. *See* Food preparation
    methods.
Body scrubbing, 34, 107, 122
Boiled Barley, 135
Boiled (Blanched) Salad, 154-155
Boiled Brown Rice, 130
*Boiled Kombu with Carrots and
    Burdock,* 170-171
Boiled Millet and Vegetables, 136
Boiling. *See* Food preparation methods.
Bok choy, 41
Bread, whole wheat sourdough, 139
Breastfeeding, 104
Brine pickles, 175
Brine Pickles, 176
Broccoli, 41, 138, 139, 149, 154, 175, 176
Broiled or Grilled White Meat Fish, 177
Brown rice, 37, 39, 106, 127-134, 142. *See
    also* Mochi.

Brown rice syrup, 134, 185, 186
Brown Rice with Millet, 129-130
Brown Rice with Pearl Barley, 129
Brussels sprouts, 149
"Bubbling spring." *See* Kidney point.
Buckwheat, 37, 39, 88, 91-92, 136, 148
Buckwheat (Kasha), 136
Buckwheat noodles. *See* Soba.
Buckwheat Soup, 148
Burdock, 41, 92, 93, 94, 121, 131, 144,
    145, 149, 150, 155, 156, 159, 167,
    169, 174
Buttercup squash. *See* Squash,
    buttercup.
Butternut squash. *See* Squash,
    butternut.

Cabbage, 41, 44, 120, 136, 137, 139, 53,
    154, 156, 158, 160, 168, 175, 185
Calcium, 22, 33
Cancer, 35, 40, 98, 107
    breast, 28, 80
    cervical, 28
    and high-fat diet, 24, 28-29, 126
    ovarian, 28, 29
    stomach, 40
    uterine, 28
Carrot and Burdock Kinpira, 159
Carrots, 41, 44, 92, 120, 121, 131, 136,
    137, 138, 139, 144, 145, 147, 149,
    150, 154, 156, 158, 159, 160, 166,
    167, 169, 171, 174, 176, 185
Cauliflower, 41, 146, 149, 175, 176
"Central field" of energy, 14
Cervix, 14, 80, 119
CFS, 115, 121. *See also* Fatigue.
Chakra (s), 5-16, 22, 23, 24, 25, 36, 41, 42,
    45, 49, 83, 85, 86, 89, 91, 98, 99, 103,
    106, 113
    fifth, 8
    first, 13, 14, 23, 38-39, 40, 41, 53, 57,
        99
    fourth, 9-10, 41, 42, 65
    second, 7, 9, 13-16, 18, 38-39, 40, 41,
        49, 65, 67, 79, 80, 83, 84
    secondary, 8-9
    seventh, 6, 15
    sixth, 6
    third, 10, 41, 49, 65
    See also Chakra energy; Chakra
        response; Stimulating the chakras.
Chakra energy, 17, 27, 31, 58, 59, 60, 75,
    77, 78, 115, 122
    cooking method influence on, 48-50
    food influence on, 22-24, 31, 35, 42,
        43-44, 46, 47, 52, 58, 92, 120
    See also Chakra(s); Chakra

response.
Chakra response, 5-19, 21, 25
Charcoal broiling. *See* Food preparation
    methods.
Chestnuts, 121, 133, 164, 180, 181, 185
Ch'i, 5
Chickpeas, 43, 121, 132, 166
Chickpeas and Vegetables, 166
Chocolate, 43, 82, 90, 91, 103, 15, 115,
    116, 119
Cholesterol, 23, 25, 26, 27, 29, 86, 90, 91,
    95, 105, 112, 116, 118, 119, 126, 177
Chronic fatigue syndrome. *See* CFS.
Clitoris, 13, 14-15, 16, 17, 23, 28, 28, 119
Coffee, 43, 48, 76, 91
Collagen, 25
Collards, 41, 153
Compatibility, 8
Complex carbohydrates, 36-37, 42, 43, 44,
    46, 47, 78, 105, 106, 121, 125, 126
Condiments, natural, 47, 122, 126,
    172-174
Condoms, 79, 81
Cooking methods. *See* Food preparation
    methods.
Corn, 37, 39, 134-135, 147
Corpora cavernosa, 90-91
"Crimes of passion," 47
"Cross-linking," 25, 26
Crown chakra. *See* Chakra, seventh.

Daikon, Kombu and Daikon Greens,
    156-157
Daikon radish, 41, 92, 120, 142, 145, 147,
    150, 153, 154, 156, 175, 176, 177,
    178, 185
Daikon-rice bran pickles, 176
Daily body scrubbing. *See* Body
    scrubbing.
Dandelion, 41
Deep frying. *See* Food preparation
    methods.
Depression, 32, 33, 114, 122
Dermoid cysts, 28, 117
Dessert(s), 178-181
Diaphragm, 81
Diet, modern day, 113-114
Diet and healthy sexuality, 87-89. *See*
    also Diet, modern day;
    Macrobiotics; Sexual problems,
    specific; Sexuality-enhancing foods.
Diet for a Strong Heart, 95
Dill pickles, 175
Disorders, gynecological, 116-119, 120,
    121
Dried Chestnuts and Dried Apples, 180
Dried Daikon, Shiitake, and Kombu, 157

Dried Tofu with Kombu and Carrots, 167
Dry roasting. *See* Food preparation methods.
Dulse, 45, 169, 173

Earth's force, 2-5, 6, 9, 25, 67, 77, 85, 88, 96, 98-99, 116, 122
 in fertilization, 18
 during foreplay, 15
 during intercourse, 15
 during labor, 14
 in massage, 15
 during orgasm, 15-18
 on sexual arousal, 14-15, 108
 on sexual organs, 13
Eggplant, 42, 92, 117
Elastin, 25
Electromagnetic fields, 49-50
Emotions, negative, 109-111, 113-114, 122
Endocrine glands, 8
Endometriosis, 119
Endometrium, 116
Energy blocks, 108-111
"Energy furnaces," 35
Epstein-Barr virus syndrome, chronic, 115
Erection, 90, 91
Estrogen, 13, 29, 80, 96, 103, 119
Eyebags, 83

Fallopian tubes, 18, 28, 83, 116, 120
Fat(s). *See* Saturated fat; Unsaturated fat.
Fatigue, 31-33, 35-36, 41, 44, 49, 65, 81, 83, 115, 122. *See also* CFS; Epstein-Barr virus, chronic.
Fatty acid, 33, 35
Fear. *See* Emotions, negative.
Fertilization, 14
Fiber, 38-39, 46, 126
Fibroid tumors, 28, 116-117, 118, 119, 121
Fish and Vegetable Soup, 150-151
Flexibility, 29, 31, 39, 42, 45, 86
Flexibility test, 30
Food preparation methods
 baking, 48-49
 blanching, 153-154
 boiling, 41, 151, 163
 charcoal broiling, 43
 deep frying, 43, 49
 dry roasting, 132-133
 grilling, 43, 49
 pickling, 151
 pressing, 151

 pressure cooking, 128-130, 161
 sauteing, 41, 151, 157-159
 shocking, 163
 steaming, 41, 48, 151
 stewing, 48
  See also Nishime cooking method; Water sauteing.
Food types
 animal, 22-23, 24, 29, 31, 32, 42, 43, 46, 78, 82-83, 84, 85, 86, 89, 90, 91, 95, 102, 103, 104, 105, 108, 111, 113, 117, 118, 119, 120, 125
 condensed, 22
 expansive, 23
 vegetable, 23, 14, 111, 125
  See also Diet and healthy sexuality; Macrobiotics; Sexuality-enhancing foods.
Foot soaking, 78
Foreplay, 101-102, 106
Framingham Heart Study, 95
Free radicals, 25
Fried Rice, 131-132
Fried Udon or Soba, 137
Fruit(s), 46, 88, 92, 106, 121, 126, 178-181
 tropical, 76, 91, 105, 115, 116, 117, 120
Fu, 127, 139-140, 143
Fu and Vegetables, 139-140

Garlic pickles, 175
Ginger compress, 97-98
Ginger pickles, 176
Ginger root, 93, 97, 138, 145, 174, 186
Glucagon, 32, 49, 104
Glucose, 10, 33, 114
Glycogen, 10, 33
Gomashio, 47, 88, 121, 136, 153, 172, 173, 174
Gomashio (Sesame Salt), 173
Gonadotropic hormones, 8
Green Lentil with Onion and Kombu, 166-167
Green nori flakes, 172
Grilling. *See* Food preparation methods.
Gynecological disorders. *See* Disorders, gynecological.

Hair loss, 82-83
Hair spiral, 6, 57-58
Hara chakra. *See* Chakra, second.
Harvard Medical School, 95
Hatcho miso. *See* Miso, soybean.
Hato mugi. *See* Pearl barley.
Heart chakra. *See* Chakra, fourth.
Heart conditions, 24, 40, 91, 96, 107, 126
Heaven's force, 2-5, 6, 9, 10, 25, 67, 77, 85, 87-88, 96, 98-99, 116, 122

during foreplay, 15
during intercourse, 15
during labor, 14
in massage, 51
during orgasm, 15-18
on sexual arousal, 14
on sexual organs, 13
Herb pickles, 175
Herpes virus, 115
High blood pressure, 40, 91, 95, 112,
    126
Hijiki 45, 121, 159, 168, 169-170
Hijiki with Onions and Lotus Root,
    169-170
Hip bath and douche, 118, 122
Hippocrates, 35
HIV, 79
Hostility. *See* Emotions, negative.
Human Sexual Inadequacy, 111
Hypoglycemia, 31-33, 44, 83, 104-106,
    114, 120, 121, 122
Hysterectomies, 28

Impotence. *See* Sexual problems,
    specific.
Infections, vaginal, 117-119, 121
Insecticide(s), 40
Insulin, 32, 33
Intercourse, 4, 14, 15, 99, 101, 102, 107,
    114, 117, 119
Intrauterine device. *See* IUD.
Irish moss, 169
Irradiated vegetables. *See* Vegetables,
    irradiated.
IUD, 79, 80-81

Japanese mountain potato. *See* Jinenjo.
Jinenjo, 41
Journal of the National Cancer Institute,
    28

Kale, 41, 153, 154
Kanten, 168
Kanten, 181
Kasha. *See* Buckwheat.
Ki, 5, 51
Ki-Kai, 14
Kidney point, 69
Kinako. *See* Soybean flour, toasted.
Kinpira, 41, 159
Koi Koku. *See* Vitality stew.
Kombu, 39, 45, 120, 121, 138, 141, 142,
    143, 145, 146, 147, 149, 150, 156,
    162, 163, 164, 166, 167, 168, 169,
    170, 173, 176, 181
Kushi Foundation, 92
Kuzu, 138, 149, 153, 178

Labia, 16, 17, 28, 118
Lancet, The, 29
Leeks, 149
Lentil Soup, 144-145
Lentil(s), 43, 121, 144-145, 162, 166, 167
Lotus root, 121, 145, 156, 169, 174
Love, 21-22
Love meditation, 11-13, 107
Low blood sugar. *See* Hypoglycemia.

Macrobiotic Diet, 40
Macrobiotic Way of Life Seminar, 92
Macrobiotics, 3, 38, 81-82, 89, 92, 95-96,
    97, 103, 105, 118, 119
    basis of, 125-126
    benefits of, 126
    categories of, 126-127
    in restoring women's vitality, 119-123
Massage, basic. *See* Shiatsu.
Masters and Johnson, 102, 103, 111
Masturbation, 103
Mekabu, 169
Meridians, 5, 6, 15, 26, 31, 34, 45, 51, 52,
    75, 77, 78, 85, 98, 102, 113, 115, 122
    bladder, 59, 60, 66-67, 70
    gall bladder, 55, 66, 70, 71
    heart, 62, 64, 65
    heart governor, 62, 64, 65
    "junction of three yin meridians," 68
    kidneys, 58, 66, 68, 70, 71, 100
    large intestine, 55, 62, 64, 65
    liver, 55, 66, 68, 70, 71, 100
    lung, 62, 64, 65
    small intestine, 55, 62, 64, 65
    spleen, 66, 68, 70, 71, 100
    stomach, 55, 56, 67, 70, 71
    triple heater, 62, 64, 65
Millet, 37, 39, 105-106, 127, 129, 136
    soup, 120, 146, 147
Millet and Corn Soup, 147
Millet Squash Soup, 146
Mirin, 185, 186
Miso, 39-40, 47, 52, 93, 141, 151, 153, 172,
    178, 186. *See also* Miso soup.
Miso barley, 141, 142, 150, 155, 166, 184
Miso, soybean, 141, 142, 172, 174
Miso bean pickles, 175
Miso pickles, 175
Miso soup, 39, 40, 120, 134, 141-142, 168
Miso Soup with Brown Rice and Daikon,
    142
Miso-Tahini Spread, 184
Mochi, 88, 134, 184
Monilial infections, 118-119
Much Depends on Dinner, 37
Mugi miso. *See* Miso, barley.
Mustard greens, 41

Musubi. *See* Rice Triangles.

National Cancer Center Research
    Institute, 40
Natto, 43
Natural birth control, 81-82
New Yorker, The, 49
Nipples, 13
Nishime, 156
Nishime cooking method, 155
Nori, 45, 130-131, 136, 146, 148, 168, 169,
    171, 174
Nori Condiment, 174
Nut(s), 46, 88, 92, 117, 121, 182

"100 meeting point," 57
Oats, 37, 39
"Ocean of electromagnetic energy," 14
Ohitashi. *See* Food preparation
    methods, blanching.
Oil sauteeing, 158
Onions, 41, 44, 131-132, 137, 140, 141,
    144, 146, 147, 148, 149, 150, 158,
    166, 167, 169, 170, 171, 172, 175,
    176, 185
Orgasm, 10, 14, 15-19, 22, 23, 99, 101,
    102, 105, 106
    multiple, 17
    See also Sexual problems, specific.
Orgasmic dysfunction, 111
Ovarian cysts/tumors, 117, 118, 119, 121
Ovaries, 13, 18, 35, 80, 83, 86, 116. *See
    also* Ovarian cysts/tumors.
Ovulation, 81

Pancreas, 32, 33, 49, 83, 104, 105
Parsnips, 185
Pearl barley, 127, 129, 147-148
Pelvic inflammatory disease. *See* PID.
Penis, 13, 15, 16, 26, 83, 90, 91, 94-95, 99,
    105
Peppers, 42, 43, 92, 117
Pickle press, 160
Pickles, 175-176
Pickling. *See* Food preparation methods.
PID, 81
Pimples, 84
Pituitary gland, 8
PMS, 28, 84
Popcorn, 183
Potatoes, 42, 43, 92, 117
Prana, 5
Premature ejaculation. *See* Sexual
    problems, specific.
Premenstrual syndrome. *See* PMS.
Preparing food. *See* Food preparation
    methods.

Pressed pickles, 175
Pressed Salad, 161
Pressing. *See* Food preparation methods.
Pressure cooking. *See* Food preparation
    methods.
Primary channel, 5-6, 8-9, 14, 15-16, 22,
    23, 24, 25, 35, 36, 38, 58, 59, 83, 85,
    89, 102
Progestogen, 80
Prostate gland, 14, 16, 17, 23, 26-27, 35,
    83, 85, 86, 91, 95, 96, 116
Prostatic concretions, 27
Prostatic enlargement, 27
Puffed wheat gluten. *See* Fu.
Pumpkin, 41, 183, 185
Pureed Squash Soup, 148-149

*Quick Tamari Soy Sauce Vegetable
    Pickles,* 175-176

Radiation effect in foods, 40
Regimen, 35
Reproduction, 45
    drug effect on, 24
Resentment. *See* Emotions, negative.
Rice, 37, 47. *See also* Brown rice; Mochi.
Rice, pounded sweet. *See* Mochi.
Rice balls, 183
Rice bran pickles, 175
Rice cakes, 183, 184
Rice rolls. *See* Sushi.
Rice Triangles (Musubi), 130-131
Rigidity, 29
Roasted Barley Tea, 187
Roasted Grain Tea, 187
Roasted Nuts, 182
Roasted Pumpkin or Squash Seeds, 183
Rye, 37, 39

Sadomasochism, 76
Salt, 47
Saturated fat, 22-23, 32, 52, 55, 71, 78, 83,
    116, 117, 118, 119, 125, 126
    effect on sexuality, 24-31, 85, 86, 90,
    102, 105, 113
Sauerkraut, 168, 175, 176
Sauteing. *See* Food preparation
    methods.
Scallion, 41, 131-132, 137, 138, 142, 143,
    144, 145, 146, 149, 172, 184
Scrambled Tofu, 167-168
Scrotum, 13
Sea palm, 169
Sea salt, 41, 47, 129, 130, 131, 135, 136,
    139, 141, 144, 146, 147, 148, 151,
    156, 163-164, 166, 173, 175, 180, 181,
    182, 186

Sea Vegetable and Roasted Sesame Seed Powders, 173-174
Sea Vegetable powder, 172, 173, 174
Sea Vegetable Powders, 173
Sea vegetables, 39, 45, 52, 89, 106, 120, 121, 126, 151, 168-171
Seasonings, natural, 47, 122, 126, 186
Sebaceous glands, 26
Secondary chakra. *See* Chakra, secondary.
Seeds, 182-183
Seitan, 88, 140, 143, 145, 149
Seitan and Onions, 140
Seitan Vegetable Stew, 149
Seminal fluid, 16, 17, 27, 79
Seminal vesicles, 16
Sensory arousal, 8
Sesame salt. *See* Gomashio.
Sesame seeds, 47, 122, 172, 173, 174
Sexual chakra. *See* Chakra, first.
Sexual organs, 10, 13, 18
Sexual problems, compensation methods
    massage, 75-76
    sadomasochism, 76
    visualization, 76
    yoga, 75
    See also Diet and healthy sexuality; Sexual problems, specific;Sexual problems and modern lifestyle.
Sexual problems, specific, 90-123
    impotence, 24, 26, 90-96, 102, 105, 114-115
    orgasm, difficulty in achieving, 23, 27-28, 107-123
    premature ejaculation, 24, 96-107, 114-115
    See also Diet and healthy sexuality; Diet, modern day; Energy blocks; Sexual problems, compensation methods; Sexual problems and modern lifestyle.
Sexual problems and modern lifestyle
    birth control, 79-82, 109
    diet, 77
    eating style, 77-78
    fabrics worn, 77
    home materials, 77
    physical inactivity, 77
    See also Diet and health sexuality; Sexual problems, compensationmethods; Sexual
Sexual vitality, assessment of
    face, 82-84
    feet, 86
    hands, 85-86
    pelvic hair, 86-87
    See also Diet and healthy sexuality.
Sexuality, healthy. *See* Diet and healthy
        sexuality.
Sexuality-enhancing foods, 36-37
    beans, 43-45
    beverages, 48
    condiments, 47-48
    fish, 46
    fruits, 46
    sea vegetables, 45
    seasonings, 47
    snacks, natural, 46-47
    soups, 39-40
    vegetables, 40-43
    whole cereal grains/grain products, 37-39
    See also Diet and healthy sexuality.
Shellfish, 177
Shiatsu, 51-73, 96, 107
    arms/hands, 62-66
    back, 59-62
    front of body, 70-72
    legs/feet, 66-70
    shoulders/neck/head, 53-59
Shiitake mushrooms, 120, 138, 143, 145, 147, 157
Shio kombu, 172
Shiso leaf powder, 172
Shocking. *See* Food preparation methods.
Simple Vegetable Stew, 150
Skin, 25-26, 102, 103, 113
Sluggishness, 23
Snacks, natural, 46-47, 183-185
Soba, 91, 137, 143
Soups, 39-40, 120, 140-151
Soy milk, 45
Soybean flour, toasted, 134
Soybean miso. *See* Miso, soybean.
Soybean Stew, 145-146
Soybeans, 40, 45, 145, 164-165. *See also* Black soybeans.
Soybeans and Kombu, 164-165
Sperm, 16, 17, 18, 27, 79, 103, 114
Spiced pickles, 175
Spices, 47, 76, 90, 103, 105
Spinach, 42
Split peas, 162
Squash, 44, 120, 136, 183, 185
    acorn, 41, 163
    buttercup, 41, 144, 148, 156, 163
    butternut, 41, 146, 156, 163
Steamed or Boiled White Meat Fish, 178
Steamed Sourdough Bread, 184
Steamer basket, 151, 184
Steaming. *See* Food preparation methods.
Stewed Fruit with Kuzu, 178
Stewing. *See* Food preparation

methods.
Stimulating the chakras, 100-101
Stomach chakra. *See* Chakra, third.
Stress, 30-31. *See also* Body scrubbing.
Stroke, 40, 91
Sugar consumption, 32-33
   complex, 33
   simple, 32, 33, 35, 36, 39, 55, 76, 82, 83, 85, 90, 103, 105, 115, 116, 117, 120
Suribachi, 155, 173, 174, 182
Sushi, 151, 171, 184
Suspicion. *See* Emotions, negative.
Sweat glands, 26
Sweet potatoes, 42
Sweet Rice with Chestnuts, 133-134
Sweet vegetable drink, 44, 48, 106, 122
Sweets, 185-186
Synthetic estrogen/progestogen pill, 79
Synthetic progestogen-only pill, 79

Tahini, 184
Takuan pickles, 175, 176
Tamari soy sauce, 39, 40, 43, 47, 52, 131-132, 134, 137, 138, 139, 141, 143, 144, 145, 148, 149, 151, 156, 159, 167, 169, 172, 174, 176, 177, 182, 183
Tamari soy sauce pickles, 175
Tan-Den, 14
Tea, 48. *See also* Bancha tea.
Tekka, 172, 174
Tempeh, 43, 88, 106, 121, 141, 143, 168
Tempeh with Sauerkraut and Cabbage, 168
Testes, 13, 15, 16, 86
Testosterone, 13, 29, 96, 102
Three-Day Tamari Soy Sauce/Vegetable Pickles, 176
Throat chakra. *See* Chakra, fifth.
Toasted Nori, 171
Tofu, 43, 45, 88, 106, 121, 138, 141, 143, 145, 167
Tomatoes, 42, 43, 92, 117
Transferase, 29
Trichomonas vaginalis, 119
Turnips, 41, 92, 120, 153, 154, 156

Udon, 127, 137, 138, 143
Udon or Soba with Tamari Soy Sauce Broth, 143
Udon with Vegetables and Kuzu Sauce, 138
Umeboshi plum, 47, 130, 141, 155, 172, 175, 186
Umeboshi-Vegetable Pickles, 175
Unsaturated fat, 23, 46, 125
Urethra, 16, 27

Uterus, 13, 14, 15, 16, 17, 18, 80, 83, 116, 119
Uvula, 10

Vagina, 13, 14-15, 16, 17, 18, 23, 81, 119
Vaginal discharge, 28, 83, 84, 117
Vaginal infections. *See* Infections, vaginal.
Vaginal secretions, 27-28, 119
Vegetable foods. *See* Food types, vegetable.
Vegetables, 39, 40-43, 46, 52, 78, 89, 126
   irradiated, 40
   leafy, 41, 48, 120-121, 158
   nightshade, 42, 92, 117
   pickled, 41, 161
   pressed, 160-161
   raw, 42, 43, 85, 90, 92, 106, 121, 160
   recipes for, 151-161
   root, 41, 88, 121, 159, 172, 175-176
   round, 41-42
   tropical, 42-43, 92
   See also Food preparation methods; Sea vegetables.
Vinegar pickles, 175
Visser, Margaret, 37
Vitality restoration in women, 119-123
Vitality stew, 92, 93-94, 122

Wakame, 39, 45, 120, 121, 141, 142, 168, 169, 171, 173
Wakame, Onion, and Carrots, 171
Water-Sauteed Vegetables, 158
Water sauteing, 158
Watercress, 41, 153, 154
Waterless cooking. *See* Nishime cooking method.
Wheat, 37, 39
Wheat gluten. *See* Seitan.
Wheat noodles. *See* Udon.
"Wheels" of energy. *See* Chakra(s).
Whipping, 76
White meat fish, 150, 177-178
Whole cereal grains/grain products, 37-39, 43, 46, 52, 78, 89, 91, 104, 105, 120, 125, 126, 127-138, 185
Whole Corn, 135
Whole wheat products, 138-140
Wood ash, 134-135

Yams, 42
Yang, 1-2, 4, 25, 32, 42, 48, 50, 80, 82, 88, 91, 99, 103, 105, 117
   in food, 22-24, 29, 31, 39, 47
   hormonal effect, 13
"Yang stress," 31
Yin, 1-2, 4, 27, 32, 36, 40, 47, 50, 80, 81,

82, 83, 84, 86, 88, 91, 99, 103, 105, 117
in food, 22, 23-24, 29, 31, 35, 39, 42, 45, 46, 48, 115, 116
hormonal effect, 13

"Yin stress," 31
Your Face Never Lies, 82

Zucchini, 42